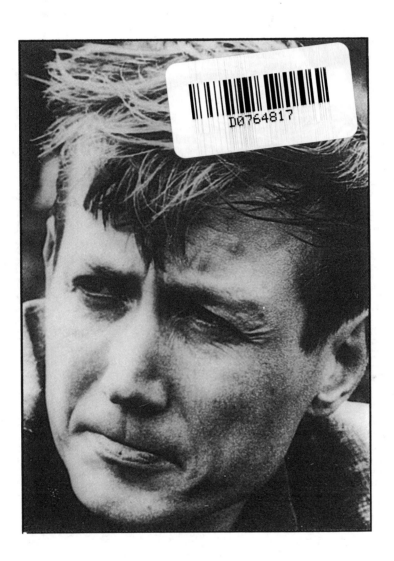

EARLY POEMS

By the same author

The Face Behind the Face
(poems)

Almost at the End
(poetry and prose)

Also available

The New Russian Poets
(bilingual anthology of Russian poetry;
selected, edited and translated by George Reavey)

YEVGENY YEVTUSHENKO
EARLY POEMS

Selected, Edited and Translated
by George Reavey

With a Preface by the Author

Marion Boyars
London • New York

This revised and enlarged bilingual edition with a preface by
Yevgeny Yevtushyenko
published in Great Britain and the United States in 1989
by Marion Boyars Publishers
24 Lacy Road, London SW15 1NL
237 East 39th Street, New York, NY 10016

This publication replaces the 1966 and 1969 bilingual collection
The Poetry of Yevgeny Yevtushenko

Reprinted 1990, 1997

Distributed in Australia and New Zealand by
Peribo Pty Ltd, 58 Beaumont Rd, Mount Kuring-gai, NSW 2080

British Library Cataloguing in Publication Data
Evtushenko, Evgenii, *1933—*
    Early poems.
    I. Title II. Reavey, George
    891.71'44

Library of Congress Cataloging-in-Publication Data
Yevtushenko, Yevgeny Aleksandrovich, 1933—
        [Poems. English. Selection]
        Early poems/Yevgeny Yevtushenko; edited and translated by George Reavey.
        Translation from Russian.
        1. Yevtushenko, Yevgeny Aleksandrovich, 1933—   —Translations,
English. I. Title.
    PG3476.E96A27   1989
    891.71'44—dc20   89-7247

ISBN 0-7145-2896-X

Printed and bound in Great Britain by
Athenaeum Press Ltd, Gateshead, England

Contents

The Cradle of Glasnost

Glasnost was not created in a test tube. Glasnost is the child our country was pregnant with even in the most terrible times, and the boots of the Cheka could not knock that child out of its womb, the way they did the child of pregnant Leningrad poet Olga Bergolts in 1937. The blows on the womb carrying unborn glasnost could not deform it before birth. The overdue child was weak and seemed in danger of not surviving. The day of Stalin's death became its birthday. But Stalin lived on after his death, and died slowly, sometimes feigning death, and still has not died completely. The tyrant's poisoned breath entered the infant's lungs, corroding them. The infant had weak muscles, fragile bones, but one thing was strong – its voice. The infant howled so loudly that it was heard not only throughout the country, but beyond its borders. The infant glasnost did not cry simply, it rhymed. The cry was poetry.

The early poetry of my generation is the cradle of glasnost. In 1953 a twenty-year-old poet from the Siberian Zima Junction began to understand two tragedies at the same time: the tragedy of World War II and the tragedy of the war Stalin and his henchmen were waging against their own people. Of course, this understanding could not be deep because of both the poet's inner immaturity and the lack of information. The understanding was only partial at first because the poet had been brought up as a child in the spirit of love for the 'best friend of Soviet children.' This poet, an adolescent, had dedicated his own naive childish poems to Stalin and wept when he died. Where did his anti-Stalinism come from then? Was it only after Stalin's death? No, no matter how paradoxical it may sound, the anti-Stalinism had existed earlier, but parallel with Stalinism in the young heart. Even children in those days could not avoid seeing the arrests, the toadying to the leader, and the terrible fear. The instinct of terror imbued children, forcing them not to think about the crimes happening all around. But the instinct of truth was stronger than the instinct of fear. Stalin's death released the instinct of truth.

When I began writing my poem *Zima Junction*, the first truth-seeking poetry after so many years of official lies, there was no Solzhenistyn, no Sakharov, no novels by Pasternak, Grossman, or Dudinstev, there were no dissidents, no abstract artists, no film *Repentance*. Akhmadulina and Voznesensky had not started publishing their poetry, the word 'jazz' was banned, and there was no private travel abroad for Soviet citizens. In 1953 I was all the dissidents rolled up into one. In 1957 I made a youthful declaration:

> Borders bother me.
>   I'm embarrassed
> not knowing Buenos Aires,
>   New York.

After the long years of Stalinism, when all the borders were closed, this was the first rebellious cry against isolation from the world. In 1960 I wrote *Babii Yar* against anti-Semitism, in 1962, *The Heirs of Stalin* with a call to throw off the oppressive shadow of the tyrant pretending to be dead.

While Stalin's heirs walk this earth,
Stalin
   I fancy, still lurks in the mausoleum.

But it does not follow that all my early poetry was thoroughly political. That would not be true. My first poems, which gained enormous reader reponse, were love poems. But even those poems, to some degree independent of my wishes, became political, since in them I defended man's great right to the personal property of his individual feelings and thoughts and rose up against the criminal collectivization of human souls. Looking back at my early poems today, I see much that is weak and naive. Some of them resemble an anthology of my lost illusions. But still there are poems that I could call an anthology of realized hopes.

When I wrote *Babii Yar* there was no monument near Kiev to the victims of fascism. Now that poem has been turned into a monument. Another early poem, *Heirs of Stalin*, is also turning into a monument for the victims of Stalinism. But the best monument to the early poems of our generation is liberation from the tyranny of censorship, from the tyranny of the observing eye of Orwell's Big Brother. And this liberation is what we call glasnost.

YEVGENY YEVTUSHENKO, December 1988
Translated by Antonina W. Bouis

Yevgeny Yevtushenko: Man and Poet

1. RUSSIA AND THE SPECTRE OF THE POET

There is something about the poet and his poetic utterance that has a terrifying effect on some Russians, and especially on the Authorities, be they Tsarist or Soviet. It is as though poetry were an irrational force which must be bridled and subjugated and even destroyed. If the critics cannot do it, then the police must try. History tells us that the lives of Russian poets have been ravaged. One need only mention the tragic fate that befell Pushkin, Lermontov, Blok, Gumilev, Yesenin, Mayakovsky, Mandelshtam and Tsvetayeva. It is as though Russia were frightened by the expanding image of its culture and, feeling threatened by the possible loss of its own simple theoretical identity, must needs shatter anything more complex as something alien to itself. This may be due to an inherent strain of puritanism. Or to the reaction of an archaic form of despotic paternalism. Perhaps, it is just the painful effect of a too sudden transition from a state of serfdom, orthodoxy, and autocracy to that of an ideologically motivated, totalitarian attempt at industrialization. Whether it is any or all of these possibilities or merely a matter of ineluctable destiny, the position of the poet in the Soviet Union, though apparently more secure in the last decade, is still highly precarious. It is still precarious because some of the younger poets and some of the hitherto muzzled older poets have become more critical and vocal, more determined to express their real feelings and to interpret the truth as they saw it. These poets have been not only anxious to voice their new-found feelings and truths, but also to condemn certain injustices and corrupt practices of the recent past when "substituting falsehood for truth, / They represented truth as falsehood," and to prevent their resurgence in the present. But it is not only a question of ideas. These poets have also been trying to rejuvenate or refresh the language of Russian poetry, which had been gravely constipated by an overdose of political clichés and slogans. They have also criticized certain of the "father images," and have made valiant efforts to enlarge their creative and cultural horizon. This, of course, they could not do without absorbing a great many "modern" elements from the West and reassessing some of the Russian writers of the Silver Age, such as Alexander Blok, Andrey Biely, and Ivan Bunin for example.

But the doctrinal purists, the dogmatists and the hacks will naturally tend to resist this healthy and inevitable trend, and maintain that so-called "ideological coexistence" between the Soviet and "bourgeois" worlds is both impossible and undesirable. The proponents of this point of view can marshall a set of propositions, apparently constant but often variable, which all fall under the general appellation of Socialist Realism (literature or art should be Socialist in content, realist in style). For the last thirty years this formula, which was first enunciated by Stalin in 1933, has been followed, bypassed, avoided, and debated. It has proved elastic: sometimes narrower; at other times, broader. But at the same time it has in practice usually served as a convenient yardstick for cutting a writer down to size or for arbitrary judgment and the condemnation of anything that seemed to endanger the closed, exclusive system of Socialist Realism. "Decadent" or "Formalist" were, and still are, the labels usually fastened to any "alien" or "undesirable" elements from outside. However, Soviet society, like any other, is subject to the laws of growth and decay, and Stalinist concepts are as perishable as any others. To interpret a rapidly changing world, a poet or artist must attune his mind and senses in part to the larger world and not merely to a closed segment of it. He must be allowed at least a large degree of artistic autonomy.

In a speech pronounced in 1921,[1] Alexander Blok, the great Russian poet, had argued that "tranquillity and freedom" were "essential to the poet in order to set harmony free." But he went on to say "they also take away our tranquillity and freedom. Not outward but creative tranquillity. Not the childish do-as-you-will, not the freedom to play the liberal, but the creative will—the secret freedom. And the poet is dying, because there is no longer anything to breathe; life has lost its meaning for him." The negative part of

---

1. *The Poet's Destination.* Speech pronounced on Feb. 11, 1921, on the occasion of the 84th anniversary of Pushkin's death.

this statement could certainly apply to poetry under the Stalin regime. It does not altogether apply in all cases to Soviet poets today; but, if we are to judge by the tone of some well-established Soviet critics of the official variety, it is not beyond the bounds of possibility that it might apply again at some time in the future. This "creative tranquillity" and this "secret freedom" are precisely what the dogmatists cannot tolerate. Boris Pasternak's sequence ("Wind: Some fragments about Blok") includes one poem that obviously refers to the above theme of Blok's, and it opens as follows:

> *Who will survive and be accepted,*
> *Who censured and accounted dead,*
> *Such is the province of our toadies—*
> *Of them alone, empowered thus.*

Significantly, the poem has been omitted from the cycle of Pasternak's 1956–60 poems included in the posthumous Soviet edition of his *Poetical Works* (1961). Yet, despite much sniping and frequent ambushes, the *avant garde* of recent Soviet poetry has succeeded in considerably expanding the frontiers of the Soviet poetic consciousness. Yevgeny Yevtushenko's *Prologue* may be regarded as an early poem of the new persuasion enunciating not only the poet's own aspirations ("I'm different . . ."), but also those of his advanced contemporaries.

It might seem unnecessary and even a pity to involve Yevgeny Yetushenko prematurely in the theme of the tragedy of the Russian poets. But Yevtushenko has shown himself well aware of this theme. He refers to it in his *A Precocious Autobiography*, touches on it very directly in the poem, "Poetry," and treats of it in a more Aesopian manner in his brutally vivid ballad, "The Execution of Stenka Razin" (1964)[2]:

> *It's worth suffering it all without tears,*
> *being racked,*
> > *broken on the wheel,*
> *if—*
> > *sooner or later—*

2. *Literaturnaya Gazeta*, March 3, 1964.

FACES
  will appear
          growing out upon
    the faces of the faceless.

More recently, on the Day of Poetry in Moscow (December 20, 1964), he read a newly written poem about Mayakovsky, a poet who has undoubtedly influenced him. He seems to imply in it that Mayakovsky (1893–1930) might have ended up in a concentration camp if he had survived until 1937, the year of the big Stalinist purges, the memory of which is still a living nightmare. That the theme of "The Poet and Russia" has also become a preoccupation with other contemporary poets is evidenced by the fact that, on the same Day of Poetry, Vladimir Tsibin also read a poem of his entitled "The Fate of All Russian Poets" in which, according to the report, he argued that, "since the early nineteenth century Russian poets have been at the mercy of the ruling powers in alternating spells of repression and liberalism."[3] In view of the recent recrudescence of this theme, one is tempted to ask what lies behind this anxiety as to the fate of the poet? Is it a mere expression of historical awareness or that of alarm as to the immediate future? It may be a form of premonition or, perhaps, a mode of vatic incantation against the possibility of such a recurrence.

However, one need not be a Cassandra. My main purpose here is to attempt a portrait of Yevtushenko as a man and to evaluate his contribution to the poetry of his day. To write about Yevtushenko is to treat not of a poet "dead and gone" and tucked away in the index files of stubborn history, but rather to discuss a poet very much alive and widely aware; a poet in the process of creating history, in so far as a poet in his work performs a creative act, interprets a mood, voices the yearnings of others, and points a direction by affirming his emotional and intellectual attitude and by using his native language in a personal and distinctive manner. The way Yevtushenko has gone about doing these things is very individual. He cannot help sharing of course a common background and certain traditions in common with some of his fellow poets. Now in his early thirties, he has shown

---

3. *The New York Times*, December 21, 1964.

in the last ten years every evidence of a steady and fruitful poetic development. Youthful and enthusiastic by temperament ("Fear not to be young, precocious . . ."), he is likewise aware of the necessity of maturing without losing his enthusiasm. (At least two poems in this book deal with this theme.) His poetry clearly demonstrates that he has moved from simpler and balder poetic statements to more complex and richer lyrical forms in the 1960's. The texture of his language has become richer and more interesting, and his lyrical quality more evident and intense. He is undoubtedly creating a poetic world of his own, a world of increasing resonance, which is the chief *raison d'être* and measure of a poet.

2. THE POET BETWEEN TWO WORLDS

For a Soviet poet of twenty-eight (1961), Yevgeny Yevtushenko had become remarkably well known, and internationally so. His international reputation, so quickly gained, may be attributed to a number of factors, since a poet rarely becomes widely famous in so short time by virtue of the quality of his poetry alone. By 1960, Yevtushenko was, to all intents and purposes, the voice of the new, post-Stalin generation in the Soviet Union. His poetry, expressive of the new aspirations, sounded a fresh and fearless note, a note to which one had become disaccustomed in Soviet poetry:

> *Frontiers are in my way.*
> > *It is embarrassing*
> *for me not to know Buenos Aires and New York.*
> *I want to walk at will through London,*
> *and talk with everyone . . .*
>
> > ("Prologue," 1953)

By 1961, he had already traveled widely (in Europe, Africa, Cuba and the U.S.A.). In doing so, he had not shut himself off in a suit of Soviet armor, as so many Soviet travelers have done for various reasons. He had absorbed and reflected on his new environment, had gone out to meet it rather than to hold it off at arm's length. He was also prepared to read his poems in public to Western audiences; and here it must be noted that, like Mayakovsky, he has a voice well geared for reading to large audiences. Then, in September 1961, he had published his "Babii Yar," a poem that raised many issues, social, political, and poetic. The most topical one was that of the persistence of anti-Semitism in the Soviet Union. Yevtushenko's direct treatment of the subject was very forthright and brave. It was this poem more than anything else that gave him such immediate worldwide publicity. "Babii Yar," a deeply felt and beautifully expressed poem, is informed with a compassion that harmonizes with its polemical intent. It was certainly a most effective poem, rousing both emotions and passions, stirring many dovecots and thus demonstrating the potential power of the poetic world. It provoked a whole barrage of rather savage attacks, of which D. Starikov's in *Literatura i Zhizn* (September 27, 1961) was perhaps the most virulent. Starikov went so far as to conclude that "what is important is that the source of that intolerable falsity with which his 'Babii Yar' is permeated lies in his obvious withdrawal from communist ideology to the positions of bourgeois ideology. This is indisputable." Before 1953, such an attack might have led to grave consequences for the poet, but the fact that he was not immediately packed off to a grimmer part of Siberia was evidence not so much of any great liberalism on the part of the ruling powers as of a more reasonable and cautious approach to the phenomena of literary life.

When I saw him in New York together with his fellow poet Andrey Voznesensky, Yevtushenko had just arrived there after a tour of the United States. It was his first visit to America, and he seemed both to enjoy it and to have a keen interest in all there was to see, from the Empire State Building to the Village beatniks. He was in no sense stuffy or dogmatic. "I was not raised on dogma," he affirms in one of his poems. Curiosity rather than dogma was a guiding trait in him. He has described this trait in another poem:

> *Little eyes like narrow slits,*
> *whence curiosity peeps out*
> *upon the world.*

To look at him, Yevtushenko is a tall young man of handsome, clean-cut, athletic appearance, who radiates energy. He impressed me as being frank and direct, as befitted a poet who, in poem after poem, has stressed the necessity of being honest, frank and fearless, and has attacked dishonesty and hypocrisy. In his earlier poems he might even have seemed to overdo this note of challenging bravado and to sound too bombastic and assertive at times. But this youthful assertiveness can be easily forgiven him when it is realized that he was fighting the battle of his generation on the poetic front against those years of mass falsification which had enveloped the Soviet people in the preceding quarter of a century. Here then was Yevtushenko, a Soviet citizen with, surprisingly, a mind of his own and little feeling of constraint. He therefore began to attract as much attention abroad as he had already at home. He was almost too self-confident, and one worried that he might get into unnecessary trouble. One could not help wondering whether he was not sticking his neck out too far. However, he seemed to bear a charmed life, and to shake off the drenching showers of periodic criticism like a duck. It was not until February-March, 1963, that he got into rather hotter water after publishing his *Autobiographie Précoce* (*A Precocious Autobiography*) in Paris. An article by him, *My Russia*, had already appeared the year before in "The London Observer," but the effect of the autobiography as a whole was, of course, greater. Yevtushenko had dared, like Boris Pasternak in the case of *Doctor Zhivago*, to publish a work of his abroad without going through the prior ritual of a censor's blessing or official approval. And just as well, because it is doubtful if that work would have appeared at all in this decade in the Soviet Union. "Autobiography" was the preserve of maturer writers, such as Ehrenburg and Paustovsky. In officious eyes, he had exceeded his prerogatives. He must be put in his place. Yevtushenko was on a reading tour at the time in Germany and France, and he was supposed to travel on to Italy and even, it is said, to Israel. He was promptly recalled to Moscow from Paris. He has since remained in Moscow, at least until the beginning of 1965. He therefore was unable to go on his second projected trip to the U.S.A. in April, 1963, when he was expected to read his poems at Princeton and other American universities. No more trips abroad for the moment, fewer Western contacts. The "frontiers," having opened, were now temporarily shut.

But this pattern did not apply to Yevtushenko alone. It also involved Andrey Voznesensky, a poet no less brave in a different fashion, and some novelists and prose writers such as Nekrasov and Aksyonov. Indeed, there was more to it than just the Yevtushenko Autobiography. It looked as if the *avant garde* writers had become too independent and modern, too critical and western-minded. They had to be given some ideological whipping in the "cleansing" vapors of the Russian, marxist, ideological Steam Bath. The ideological re-assessment begun in October, 1962, now took on an increasingly sharp form and developed into a running debate which continued hammer and tongs into June, 1963. There had been Khrushchev's crude outburst against the "modern" artists, such as the sculptor Neizvestny, who were exhibiting at the Moscow Manege in December, 1962, and his apparently uncompromising speech of March 8, 1963. There had been speeches by L. F. Ilyichev, who headed the ideological branch of the Central Committee. And there had been a whole plethora of speeches in writers' organizations, as well as a flood of articles in the dailies and periodicals. The substance of the official propositions was much the same. It boiled down to a reassertion of the controlling principles of Socialist Realism, the rejection of the possibility of "ideological coexistence," and sharp criticism of individual writers. The following from a speech by S. P. Pavlov, the first secretary of the Young Communist organizations, will suffice as an example: "There is scum in every flood. It is also present in our young literature. Especially in the work of Yevtushenko, Voznesensky, Okudzhava . . . We're ashamed of their posturing and vanity. We're ashamed that, blinded by their fame, these young people have begun to bite at the most primitive bait. And our ideological enemies are big specialists in the matter of baits . . ." Despite all the thunder and browbeating, the bark proved worse than the final bite. A large enough number of writers put up a show of resistance, and a sort of *modus vivendi* was arrived at for the time being. But the freedom to travel abroad was very definitely curtailed in the case of certain poets and novelists who were being grilled—those who had exhibited too much individual conscience, as Nekrasov had also done in his articles about his trip to the USA. Yevtushenko was even refused permission to travel to Poland, where he was expected to read his poetry. A *Pravda* editorial of January 9, 1965, reissued a warning against "formalism" and "digressions from realism," and asserted that "there cannot be any peaceful coexistence in the ideological field." This renewed insistence on the same point may well be due to the persistence of the so-called "digressions" or "deviations." It may also have been the result of the nature of some of the poems which had been read in December on Poetry Day.

3. ORIGINS, YOUTH AND EARLY POETRY

Yevgeny Yevtushenko is proud to call himself a Siberian. "I am of Siberian breed," he proclaims in the opening line of a 1954 poem. I have met other Russians who were also proud of their Siberian origins. This claim has a special connotation in Russia. A "Siberian" regards himself as somewhat superior to an ordinary Russian. He likes to think of himself as bigger, tougher and, above all, *freer*. This may strike us as paradoxical, since Siberia has also been notorious for its prisons and concentration camps. But Siberia was also a land of frontiersmen and pioneers, as well as a Tsarist, and then Soviet dumping ground for political exiles and rebels (the Decembrists and recalcitrant intellectuals; Dostoyevsky, Babel, Mandelshtam). Many of these exiles settled permanently in various parts of Siberia. There is therefore a certain tradition of intellectual liberty in Siberia. Moreover, the Siberian peasant was never a serf as he had been in Muscovy.

Thus, Yevgeny Yevtushenko was born at Stantzia Zima (Winter Station) on July 18, 1933. Zima Station is a settlement or small provincial town situated on the famous Transiberian railway in the Irkutsk region, near Lake Baikal. Yevtushenko has immortalized his birthplace in many poems, and particularly in his "Zima Station" (1956). Zima is also the scene of certain other poems, such as "The Concert," "Babushka," and "Again at Zima Station." In the latter poem we find the following playful but affectionate description:

> *Zima! a station small with palisade,*
> *half-a-dozen drooping trees,*
> *and a kholhoz woman with porkers in a sack . . .*

Zima might indeed appear to be a "provincial hole" to some chance traveler like the one bitingly described in "Again at Zima Station," but Yevtushenko has shown himself very attached to it. He feels the need to return there from time to time for spiritual refreshment:

> *when have I not adored you, Station Zima,*
> *as Yesenin did his peasant mother?! . . .*
>
> *Whenever I come back to you, Zima,*
> *I always feel as though reborn . . .*

He still has relatives there—mainly uncles and aunts.

The name Yevtushenko is Ukrainian. His paternal great-grandfather was a peasant from the province of Zhitomir who had been exiled to Siberia for burning a landowner's house, a not infrequent act in the pre-revolutionary days. His grandfather, Yermolay Yevtushenko, was a soldier who during the Revolution and the civil war became a leader in the East Siberian peasant movement. He then rose to the rank of commander in the Red Army. In the light of Yevtushenko's attitude to the Russian Revolution as an ideal and of his hatred for the abuses of Stalinism, it is significant to note that his grandfather was both an early enthusiastic supporter of the Revolution and, later, an innocent victim of the Stalin purges. The arrest, deportation and utter disappearance of his grandfather, though this fact was at first concealed from the young boy, must eventually have been a great shock to Yevtushenko, who had hitherto tended to accept the image of Stalin as something sacrosanct. His disillusion with this aspect of his past was further intensified after Khrushchev's "secret speech" at the famous Twentieth Congress (1953). Soon after he began writing his long poem "Zima Station," in which he reviewed and reassessed the past and present (his own), and tells us something about the Yevtushenkos.

Yevtushenko's father was a more intellectual type. A steady reader of literature and poetry, a geologist by profession, he introduced his son to serious reading at an early age. The family, however, split up before the end of the war. The father remarried, and pursued his geological work in Kazakhstan. Yevtushenko's mother Zinaida was born (1910) in Siberia of Latvian parents. His Latvian grandfather, Rudolph Gangnus, a mathematician and writer of geometry textbooks, was also arrested as a Latvian spy during the purges on a trumped-up charge. As a result of the divorce of his parents, Yevtushenko was brought up by his mother and, for a time, by relatives. In a number of poems Yevtushenko has testified to his regard and affection for his mother. In "I Congratulate You, Mamma," he writes that she had given him "neither fame, nor riches" but a "hard, proud faith in the Revolution" and "the ability not to fear."

The young Yevgeny or "Zhenia," as he is more familiarly called, did not spend all of his early youth in Zima Station. In the late 1930's his mother took him to live in Moscow. Then came war. In the autumn of 1941, Zhenia was among the many children evacuated from Moscow. At the age of eight he went back to live with his uncles and aunts in Zima Station, and there he stayed for three years. Yevtushenko later recorded the atmosphere of those years, and especially of "the terrible year '41" in Siberia in his poem "Weddings" (1955) and certain other poems. He could never forget those one-night weddings of the Siberian recruits who were rushed to the front to save besieged Moscow. From this poem we also learn that the young "Zhenia" was already a "folk dancer of repute," who could "stamp his feet and bend his knees." The moral he draws at the end of the poem, "My heart's not in the dance, / but it's impossible not to go on dancing," would also apply to other difficult moments in life and especially to his more critical days as a poet. Zima Station, besides serving him as a background for country characters, landscape and forest scenes (the famed Siberian Taiga), also proved a rich source of folklore and folk song, in which the poet-to-be developed an early interest. Indeed, he has been able to make good use of the folk element in a number of his poems, as well as in his poetic language. Some of his poems of 1963–64 are very Siberian and show the impact of folklore. Like Sergey Yesenin, the peasant poet from Ryazan, Yevtushenko has preserved a deep feeling for his native soil and landscape. But he is not only a country poet; he is a city poet too. He has, indeed, described himself as half and half peasant and intellectual.

In 1944, before the war ended, he was brought back to Moscow where he continued his rather desultory education which included, as he tells us, a period of close and dangerous contact with the life of the streets. He was belligerent and fought the toadies. He had difficulties at school and was even expelled from one. But he survived the dangers and hardships, and was writing poems in the midst of it all. Life in Moscow was hard during the war years, for his mother made only a marginal living as a singer in a cinema and then a minor employee. At the age of fifteen, Yevtushenko went off and joined his father for a time in Kazakhstan and got a job, first as a handyman and, then, as a collector with a geological expedition in the Altai region. It is not surprising that he should have entitled his first published volume of poems "Prospectors of the Future" (1952).

There was a moment when, on his return to Moscow, Yevtushenko almost decided to become a professional footballer. But after publishing his first poem, in 1949, in *Soviet Sport*, he opted for literature. Soon people, who thought he had a future as a poet, began to encourage him to go on writing. Eventually he was given a chance to study at the Gorky Literary Institute in Moscow, the official training ground for many Soviet poets and novelists. In the early 1950's he began to be published more widely in the established literary papers and magazines. It was during this period that he met and married his first wife, Bella Akhmadullina, a talented poet of Tartar origin. His first book was followed in rapid succession by five others: *Third Snow* (1955), *The Highway of Enthusiasts* (1956), *Promise* (1957), *The Bow and the Lyre*, and the culminating volume of this series, *Poems of Various Years* (1950). *Poems of Various Years* may be said to mark in a sense the completion of Yevtushenko's initial phase as a poet at the age of twenty-five. In the poems of his first creative decade Yevtushenko had shown himself to be a poet of concentrated aim and wide interests. He was still a youthful poet, whose themes and enthusiasm could generate increasing excitement. He had a distinctive and attractive lyrical note of his own. He had studied rhyme and produced original effects. He was a voice, but he had not yet achieved a great deal. His main themes as behoved a lyrical poet were nature ("Nature requires that we love her"), love, and himself. Then, to these he added a belief in poetry, a faith in the Russian people, a love for his native land, and various patriotic motifs. He also reaffirmed his belief in the original ideals of the Revolution, and condemned the corruption of those ideals. Yevtushenko, we find, is always careful to distinguish between the long suffering and much abused "Russian people" and the race of bureaucrats or careerists who swarmed like locusts over the land:

> *It seems*
> > *we are divorced from nature,*
> *and have unlearnt*
> > > *to breathe in branches.*
> *But in us love*
> > *is alive to all that's Russian,*
> *green,*
> > *dewy,*
> > > *and fragrant.*

The tone and feeling of the new generation of Soviet poets is well expressed in the following lines of Yevtushenko's from "There's Something I Often Notice" (1953):

> *Let us share our anxieties together,*
> *discuss between us, tell others too,*
> *what sort of men we can't be any longer,*
> *what sort of men we now desire to be.*

There is something these poets must share, something they must break away from, and something they must strive for. In "Zima Station" (1956), the long poem which Yevtushenko had been writing since 1953, the poet treats not only of himself, his background, the family history and nature, and the early days of the Revolution, but also of the moral consequences of political corruption and of the shocking revelations that followed Stalin's death ("Now that the doctors have proved innocent . . ."). As a result of all this, the poet, who had previously "had no doubts," now "suddenly felt it necessary to answer these questions for myself." The time had come to do some independent thinking rather than to rely on rationalizations and harmonious solutions to all apparent problems.

The year 1953 had helped to transform Yevtushenko. Until then, though a poet of promise, he was still far from realizing in deadly earnest all the implications of the poet's vocation. He had been apt, he admits, to blink an eye on occasion when a careerist editor would insert a line or two in praise of Stalin in a poem and thus connive at the proliferation of what came to be labelled as "the cult of the personality." However, a dawning sense of responsibility made Yevtushenko adopt a firmer attitude, and he began to make a point of insisting on poetic integrity. He also wrote more boldly and touched upon issues which had, until then, been kept under the surface. These issues may be summed up as the necessity of admitting the horrible mistakes of the 1930–40's and insisting on the truth being told. When they were brought out into the open at last, they naturally appeared controversial and, therefore, caused a great deal of displeasure in certain circles:

> *It will go hard with me at times,*
> *and they will say:*
> > *"He'd better hold his tongue!"*

In Soviet conditions these issues could not help but assume at times a sharp political edge even though they were in the circumstances the subject matter of legitimate poetical expression. The issues Yevtushenko began to raise in his poetry were not something purely subjective, though his manner of doing so was individual, but rather reflected the wider longings and aspirations of that younger generation which was fated to apprehend the new "atomic world" of the 1950's. In one of its main aspects this new generation of "sons" represented an inevitable and too-long-delayed revolt against many representatives of the previous bootlicking generation of the "fathers," who had been caught up in and morally devasted by the world of Stalinist machinations. It was a confrontation as poignant and as unavoidable as that depicted by Turgenev in his *Fathers and Sons*, with this difference, that now, a hundred years later, it was the turn of the younger idealists to attack the established generation of the now compromised cynical radicals. The very concept of the Revolution was now at stake. What had been besmirched, was now to be purified, re-defined, and brought up-to-date. The Revolution was something more than the arbitrary will of one man or of a Stalinist-type bureaucracy. This was not the only aspect involved in what was a deep emotional and critical change going on in the psyche of the Russian people. But, as far as the conflict between sons and fathers was concerned, it is not surprising, perhaps, that the "fathers" officially tried to prevent the rift from growing or even showing and being publicly admitted. Khrushchev had laid it down: in Soviet Socialist society there are no contradictions between generations. There is no father-and-son problem in the old sense. In other words, there has been a steady attempt to hush up or to conceal its very existence, even though Yevtushenko, Voznesensky, and other young poets and writers have been constantly criticized for being "immature" and for not listening to their more experienced "elders." ("He's so young . . . There are older men about. What's he after in such a hurry?") The official critics stress this point again and again. On the other hand, Vasily Aksyonov, a writer, in an interview printed in the Warsaw *Polytika* (Spring 1963) can state: "The characteristic of the Soviet youth of our days consists in that it rejects the traditions and the manner of life, which had become established in the days of the cult of personality. The young people reject all this both as a whole and in each particular, and this fact disturbs certain representatives of the other generation."

The function of poetry as practised by Yevtushenko could not be merely negative and critical, social and political, ethical and moralizing ("forgiving no evil even if it does some good"). By its nature, poetry is the language of the emotions and feelings, a form of aesthetical affirmation and ideal statement. The poets of the new generation had therefore to reaffirm a number of beliefs of an emotional and aesthetic kind as well as their social ideals. They had to assert a renewed belief in the integrity and validity of poetry itself, in the value of the word and the possibilities of language and diction, in the right to experiment with form and to adapt it to a new content. In so far as there has been lyrical revival[4] in the past decade, helped on, it is true, by older poets such as Boris Pasternak, Nikolai Zabolotzky, and Leonid Martynov, and in so far as the poets of this revival with Yevtushenko in their van have been both critical and affirmative, it is not surprising that their promise of a new world should have evoked a keen response from an increasing audience.

4. See *Survey* No. 46, London: January 1963. Pierre Forgues, "The Young Poets." This article gives a general survey of the poetic revival.

The best indication of the genuine popularity of the new poetry was in the phenomenal jump in the circulation of books of poetry and in large attendance at poetry readings. In the case of Yevtushenko, the rise has been from earlier editions (in 1959), of 20,000 to editions, in 1962, of 100,000 copies; in that of Voznesensky, from 5,000 (in 1960) to an edition of 60,000 copies in 1964.

In Yevtushenko's "Prologue," a sort of youthful, lyrical manifesto poem, there is, besides the theme of the "frontiers," an insistence on a freer, more embracing art and the need for diversity:

> *I want art to be*
> *as diverse as myself* . . .

He also insists on "movement," "ardor," "freshness," and, above all, on the joy of living. This almost Renaissance sense of joy and exuberance is typical of the poet. It is also exemplified in the poem "Moscow Freight Station." In Yevtushenko there is, on the one hand, an all-embracing abundance of spirit; on the other, an undertone of anxiety, strain, and suppressed anguish ("the warring strains in all my moods"). This duality, which has often proved to be the dynamic force of poetry, represents the emergence of a new and more subjective element in later Soviet poetry. This element had always been present in Russian poetry, and had certainly been an integral part of the poetic worlds of Yesenin and Mayakovsky, but diversity and duality have always been considered dangerous elements from the standpoint of the advocates of Socialist Realism. These latter would argue, as Khrushchev did, that "Some people are trying to push us on to the road of ideological coexistence and to palm off the rotten idea of absolute freedom." Or, to put it in another way, as Alexander Chakovsky, the new editor of *Literaturnaya Gazeta*, was quoted as saying[5] during his visit to New York: "We are a goal-oriented society; we will not stand by and let these things harm us. We have a definite line in art—not *laisser-faire*, not *laisser-passer*." But it is also clear that most of these statements are made by party executives and party critics, and that fundamentally they have little or nothing to do with literature. However, since

---

5. "Art for Marx's Sake." *N.Y. Times Magazine Section*, December 20, 1964.

poets will be poets, and party men will be ideologists and politicians, the twain shall never quite meet in the best of worlds. Thus, tension is bound to persist, sometimes less, sometimes more acute; and the presence of this strain must therefore be suffered like some recurring, incurable ache.

4. POET AND TRAVELER 1960–62

In 1960, the year of Boris Pasternak's sudden death, Yevgeny Yevtushenko was already a maturer and more confident poet. He was ready for bigger and more ambitious tasks. He was about to make the acquaintance of Europe and the United States. He was going to enlarge his horizon and to tempt fortune. He was, indeed, about to become internationally known. And he was also about to discover the limitations which would be applied from the outside upon his dynamic will. Yevtushenko's work and activities from 1960 to early 1965 may be divided into two main phases: the first lasted up to March 1963, when, despite much criticism, he seemed comparatively free to move about, travel abroad, and publish some of his most controversial poems, such as "Babii Yar" and "The Heirs of Stalin" and "Conversation with an American Writer." He even published an autobiography in Paris, which had not been previously submitted to the Soviet censors. In addition, he was able to publish in Moscow three volumes of his poetry, and to get printed in a wide range of Soviet papers, periodicals and magazines. The second phase, during which every effort was made to make him less independent and to recant, has continued with a variation of pressures into 1965. This last phase differs from the previous one in that Yevtushenko has now been confined in the Soviet Union and has not published a single book in the past two years. It is true, however, that he has been able to have some of his new cycles of poems printed in the magazines after about a six-month gap in publication.

In his volume *Yabloko* (*Apple*),⁶ published at the end of 1960, Yevtushenko had printed such poems as "Freshness," "Our Mothers Depart," "Moscow Freight Station," "Humor," "The Cocks," to mention only five of the forty-two poems included in the book. These

---

6. Also the name of a popular Russian song.

poems evidence a wide variety of theme. Some are occasional, others reflective; some more programmatic, others purely lyrical. The poet's moods vary from sheer exuberance to sadness. There are poems about love and loss, work and pleasure, art and politics, Samarkand and the Volga. There are also poems about the young people of his generation, about their loves and personal frustrations. The recurring theme of love and personal relations is a brave new one in the Soviet Union. In "Humor," Yevtushenko touches boldly on a theme with political overtones—the power of humor or wit in the struggle against tyranny or absolute authority.

> *They tried to murder humor,*
> *but he thumbed his nose at them.*

He was able to revive this theme in a different context in a later poem, "Nefertiti" (1964), written after his encounter at the Manege Art Exhibition, in which the poet argues for the more enduring quality of a work of art (in this case the bust of Nefertiti) as against the more impermanent authority of political power:

> *. . . when, in nature, authority comes face to face*
> *with beauty, its value depreciates.*

In "The Cocks," a poem written while Yevtushenko was vacationing in Koktebel in the Crimea, the crowing cocks "summon us to stop from yielding." These cocks therefore become symbols of an "awakening." When the students in his youthful and lively "Moscow Freight Station" settle down to talk on the platform, they very significantly discuss "cybernetics, Mars, and Remarque." Nothing could better illustrate the temper of the new Soviet generation. A decade or two ago they would have certainly been discussing Marx rather than Mars. As for Remarque, his appeal to Soviet youth is still regretted by the more orthodox critics. In another poem the poet calls for "freshness" in "music and language" among other things. Such a plea in the West might seem justifiably appropriate and innocuous, but Yevtushenko intends it in dead seriousness as a protest against the weight of the musty past of ideologically congealed art. "Freshness" in this context is a battle cry, though very gently and lyrically expressed in this instance. The same point is made in a more direct and militant, though witty, poem, "Rockets and Carts" (1960), in which the poet contrasts a need for a new rocket-like art with the persistence of "cart-like" novels and operas and, no doubt, poems. A statement of this sort rings like a challenge and is obviously aimed at "careerist" authors and artists. In an earlier poem, "A Career" (1957), Yevtushenko had already made it abundantly clear that he was for Galileo as against any form of Inquisition and the type of careerist who plays it safe, and he was also for Van Gogh as against the *pompier* type of artist. "We need no pedantic light," he says. In this stand Yevtushenko is by no means alone. Andrey Voznesensky, for example, has made the same point in his more complex poem, "The Parabolic Ballad" (1960), in which he uses Gauguin as the symbol of creative unorthodoxy. It is, perhaps, all rather like Victor Hugo attacking the moribund classical establishment of his day. But the Soviet "establishment" has still a lot of bite left, because it controls the greater part of the critical apparatus. In the situation of Soviet poetry, it would seem a creative and healthy sign to have a point to make, especially if that point is concerned with the defense and possibility of being creative. The danger of course is in overdoing the manifesto element at the expense of the magic of poetry. But if Yevtushenko is at times the moralist, he is far from being entirely so; and the lyrical quality of his poetry has been growing richer rather than poorer.

For Yevtushenko, as well as Voznesensky, 1961 was to be a year of venture and adventure. Traveling together, the two poets visited the United States in April for the first time. That the visit had an impact on both of them is evidenced by the fact that they wrote a number of poems on American themes. Voznesensky wrote a whole cycle of poems under the title of *Triangular Pear* (1962), his most interesting effort so far, because he also attempted to develop new forms. Yevtushenko's poetic reactions in some half-a-dozen poems were more occasional. If the two poets are to be compared, one might say that Voznesensky writes less and more concentratedly, progressively paying more attention to the image as a vehicle of modern sensibility. In his language, too, he employs to a greater extent a variety of modern technical words, thus giving his poetry a particularly modern flavor. He is more of an urban poet than Yevtushenko. Yevtushenko has potentially a wider range of interests, greater facility and a more public presence. For all the increasing differences between them, Yevtushenko and Voznesensky have much in common. They complement each other. There seems to be no point in saying, as some people do, that one poet is "better" than the other. Each of them is making a valuable contribution in his own way. Yevtushenko also paid a visit to Cuba, a visit he was to repeat the following year. The result was a body of poems evoking his impressions of that revolutionary island. He returned to the Soviet Union via Paris. The year before, he had already traveled to England, France, Catalonia, Africa, and even Bulgaria. All these trips have been recorded in poems. It was in September, 1961, after his return from abroad, that Yevtushenko published his internationally famous poem "Babii Yar." He had at first some difficulty in getting it accepted, but finally, upon appeal to the highest authority, the poem appeared in *Literaturnaya Gazeta*. It was a very brave and bold attempt to bring out into the open many of the festering sores in the Soviet body politic.

The years 1960–61 were of tremendous importance to Yevtushenko both from the standpoint of the development of his poetry and from that of the growth of his popularity. He published his next two volumes in editions of 100,000 each. *A Wave of the Hand (Vzmakh Ruki)*, which appeared in the spring of 1962, is a volume of 352 pages. Obviously not all of the poems in it were new. The book is divided into three sections: *Poems About Abroad, Let Us Be Great!* and *Morning Poems*. The latter contains sixty-five poems, representing a selection of his earlier work from 1952 to 1960. They are mainly the sort of poems that have already been discussed. In the twenty-eight *Poems About Abroad* Yevtushenko has collected the poems he wrote about foreign countries—England, France, Catalonia, Bulgaria, Ghana, Liberia, Togo. These poems are, for the most part, the immediate impressions of a traveler, a sort of diary in verse with here and there a moral drawn or an injunction made. Ten of the poems are about Paris or French themes; four on Cuba; and eight on Africa. There is only one poem, and that a satirical one, "Uriah Heap," about England, and in it Yevtushenko describes a brush he had with a customs officer. Two poems are on American themes: one about Hemingway, whom he apparently saw in passing at a restaurant at an airfield in Copenhagen; and the other about his visit to Harvard in 1961, in which, after waxing lyrical about the similar nature of Russian and American nightingales, he makes a plea for friendship between the two countries. Both these poems have, it seems to me, a solider lyrical strength than the other pieces. The Hemingway poem is not just accidental. For over a decade Hemingway has been to Yevtushenko not only an heroic figure, but also a model for writing—a model in the sense of compression, terseness and virility. In the middle section of fifty-seven poems, *Let Us Be Great!*, Yevtushenko has gathered those poems which have political overtones, such as "Envy," "A Career," "Rockets and Carts" and "Humor," which have been discussed or quoted elsewhere. *Let Us Be Great!* is something like a motto for Yevtushenko. It can be interpreted as a sort of heroic challenge—let us try and live on a higher ethical plane—a very necessary ideal after the low level reached during the Stalinist rule of distrust and betrayal.

Yevgeny Yevtushenko's next book, *Tenderness (Nezhnost)*, followed quickly on *A Wave of the Hand*. This book was published in the autumn of 1962, soon after Voznesensky's *Triangular Pear*. In outward appearance both these books looked very different from any previous book published by their authors. They had abstract jackets of modern geometric design suggesting the art of Mondrian. In fact, a Soviet critic could easily have labelled them "formalistic." They reminded one of the days of Mayakovsky's *Lef* and the experiments of the Soviet 1920's, which had been condemned since the early thirties. These books looked different, modern and challenging. Even more surprising was that 100,000 copies of *Tenderness* had been printed. It should be noted that Yevtushenko had been abroad prior to the publication of this book. He had been to Cuba again, and had also spent almost a month in England in April-May, reading his poems in London, Oxford and Cambridge, and elsewhere. This was the third year in succession that he had spent some months abroad. He was indeed becoming almost a permanent news item in the international press. Inwardly, *Tenderness* is divided into two sections. The last section of twenty-two poems is entirely devoted to Cuban themes. The Cuban poems of *A Wave of the Hand* had now grown into a whole cycle. At least two poems, "The American Cemetery" and "The Hemingway Hero" also touch on the American theme largely through Hemingway. In the former poem, Yevtushenko opens as follows:

> *The American cemetery,*
> *abandoned by people,*
> *gazes sadly and sorrowfully,*
> *as though asking for love.*

Having described the atmosphere of the cemetery and having quoted some complaints about the United States voiced by a Cuban woman, Yevtushenko recalls Hemingway:

> *He died, but his deathless lines*
> *teach us to live greatly,*
> *but have we, America,*
> *ever called him "gringo"?*
>
> *A Russian, I would very much like*
> *with all my life and all the destiny*
> *of flights, construction and creation,*
> *America, to be together with you.*
>
> *I wish the word "gringo" to be*
> *cleanly erased from the dictionary,*
> *that all nations might respect*
> *the graves of their sons.*

In the second poem, Yevtushenko meets and talks to the old fisherman Anselmo who had served as the prototype for Hemingway's *The Old Man and the Sea.* It should be borne in mind that, to a young Soviet poet of Yevtushenko's generation, revolutionary Cuba exercises great fascination. All the more so for Yevtushenko, who has been so critical of post-revolutionary corruption in his own Soviet motherland. It is very natural for him to seek some source of purer expression of the revolutionary ideal elsewhere:

> *Revolution*
> *   is a harsh business,*
> *but it's no gloomy thing,*
> *   the devil take it!*

> *Revolution,*
>> *do away with all things*
> *that are officious and for parade!*

The first section of *Tenderness* contains seventy-four poems, almost all of them new. They cover a wide range of subject matter. There are new poems about Paris and New York ("Girl Beatnik" and "Monologue of the Beatniks," which are better poems than the earlier "Angry Young Men"), several polemical poems, and a number of poems about women, as well as a variety of others. In the polemical poems, as in "Honey," Yevtushenko directs his attack against the inhumanity of a wartime official figure ("he's still alive"), and in "Conversation with an American Writer," written in New York, he claims to speak "all on my mind" and delivers a very forthright frontal assault on "the cowardice" of certain "colleagues":

> *Yes, I defended men of talent,*
> *branding the hacks, the would-be writers.*

No doubt "Babii Yar" should have been, and would have been, included in this volume, too, if it had been found possible to reprint it. In certain other poems such as "Women," "Saleswoman of Ties," and "The Woman and the Sea," Yevtushenko is preoccupied with the nature and character of women. In "The Woman and the Sea," he expresses his admiration for a woman who shows herself determined and strong:

> *In moments of stress,*
> *complication and distress,*
> *when out of cowardice*
> *we begin to squirm,*
> *then women*
>> *of vigor,*
> *who like to laugh,*
> *will remind us*
> *we*
>> *are men!*

There is likewise compassion, as in the earlier poem "I Don't Understand," for women who have to bear with life's miseries:

> *A saleswoman with straggly curls,*
> *with inept but darling hands . . .*
> *I now stared hard,*
> > *and pain pinched my heart,*
> *and pity, you must know,*
> > > *pure pity*
> *I felt for her clean, exhausted hands . . .*

This note of compassion for women is also characteristic of Boris Pasternak—in his poetry and *Doctor Zhivago*. Yevtushenko has always had a sympathetic eye for the ordinary man and the underdog. He has even been reproached for this. But it is his way of saying that he is aware of the suffering of the Russian people as he certainly is in "Honey." This note of universal compassion may explain the title of his book— *Tenderness*. In this connection, his attitude may be defined as that of tenderness towards people and harshness towards the selfish bureaucrats. It may, indeed, be recalled that, in answer to a questionnaire, Yevtushenko once wrote in *Voprosy Literaturi* that there should be only two Ministers in the future ideal Communist State: Tenderness (*Nezhnost*) and Truth (*Pravda*). There are other poems of his such as "Hail in Kharkov" and "The Railing" which, in their buoyant and boisterous word play, their alliteration and assonance, remind one of the sound and movement of Pasternak's earlier poetry. "The Railing" is an elegiac poem that might well refer to Pasternak and his grave in Peredelkino—"His was a large, childlike smile / upon the face of a martyr of this age." And very like Pasternak's, too, is the rushing sound of:

> *The peace of ponds,*
> > *the crump of crashing icefloes,*
> *the hazard of bazaars,*
> > *the integrity of temples,*
> *gardens in full blow, and clumps of cities.*

In "Hail in Kharkov" Yevtushenko expresses pure delight in the sound of words, the sounds that convey in a sort of staccato dancing rhythm the thrashing sound of hail. By the end of the poem, in the Yevtushenko manner, the hail also becomes the symbol for a certain natural freedom in which those young of heart can exult:

> *All who are young*
> *are glad of hail.*

But the poet also draws attention to another sort of hail through which he has to walk:

> *the hail of gibes,*
> *of crafty slanders,*
> *which assail me on every side.*

In the end, the poet interprets "hail is / a reward / to those who fear no barriers."

In early 1965, *Tenderness* was still the last volume of Yevtushenko's poetry to have been published in the Soviet Union. As from late 1962, we have available only those new poems of Yevtushenko which have appeared in the dailies, periodicals and magazines. A notable poem of his, "The Heirs of Stalin," was printed only in *Pravda* (October 21, 1962). It obviously required the authority of that daily for the poem to be printed at all, for in it Yevtushenko very openly raised the question of the persistence and survival of a Stalinist mentality and a body of Stalinist supporters who were still eager to seize power. The poem is frankly anti-Stalinist. It also intrudes into the sphere of foreign politics, since it contains a direct reference to Enver Hoxha of Albania and a hidden allusion to the Chinese problem or, rather, to the pro-Stalinist attitude of the Chinese Communist Party, which is a matter of grave concern to the Kremlin. Yevtushenko urges vigilance to prevent any possible resurrection of Stalinism—"stop Stalin from ever rising again. . . ." The political aspect of this poem is clear enough. What is not so clear is why and how a Soviet poet could have intervened in such a delicate matter. The imprimatum of *Pravda* in this case indicates official sanction and perhaps even the backing of Mr. Khrushchev himself. If so, Yevtushenko at that moment seemed to be in an extraordinary position; he spoke out, he was much attacked, yet he could go on speaking out and raising the most provocative issues. It seemed, indeed, as if he could dare anything. He had reached a height of eminence where he could even write in his "Poetry":

> *"The poet*
> > *is like Kutuzov the clearsighted . . .*
> *They slander him from left*
> > *and right,*
> *but he looks down on the liars with contempt."*

But "The Heirs of Stalin" was more than just a political poem. It also spoke of the hurt and damage that had been done by Stalin—the distrust he had sown, the prison camps he had filled, the youth he had perverted, the people's good he had neglected, the innocent men he had jailed. In this sense Yevtushenko was speaking both to and for his generation. The poem is also interesting from the purely poetical point of view. Its tone is grave and sustained—ironically enough, it is the tone of an elegy which unexpectedly turns into a denunciation. The imagery is often arresting: the surprising image of the telephone in Stalin's coffin is worthy of Mayakovsky. Throughout the poem there is a certain amount of alliteration effectively used:

> *Mute was the marble.*
> > *Mutely glimmered the glass.*
> *Mute stood the sentries,*
> > *bronzed by the breeze.*

As in "Babii Yar," Yevtushenko here succeeds in writing a powerful and aesthetically satisfactory poem. The poem is about Stalin, but not about Stalin in the old, mechanical, obsequious manner, to which the poet Pavel Antokolsky referred when he wrote in 1956:

> *We, laureates of prizes*
> *given us in his name,*
> *had all walked in silence*
> *through a time now dead.*

And, finally, it is not really a poem about Stalin, but one about the aspirations of the new generation, who do not want to be trampled upon and betrayed.

5. THE TURN OF THE WHEEL. THE POETS ARE RESTRICTED

But contrary forces were now at work. Certain elements within the Party were perturbed by the independent attitudes and the unbridled directions which the younger writers were taking. By December of 1962, the criticism was mounting and becoming more official. There was even a verbal passage at arms in public between Khrushchev and Yevtushenko. Whatever the outcome was to be, neither Yevtushenko, nor Voznesensky, seemed unduly disturbed as yet. They went off again to the West of Europe. In early February, 1963, Yevtushenko had arrived in West Germany on a reading tour for the first time there. He read his poems in Hamburg and elsewhere to enthusiastic audiences of students. *Stern* magazine featured him largely in its pages. From Germany he proceeded to Paris where he gave a number of readings which were also widely reported. There, on February 18, he read the poem entitled "The Dead Hand of the Past," which opens as follows:

> *Someone is still living as of old,*
> *attempting to knife whatever's new.*
> *Someone still glares in the Stalin manner,*
> *looking at young men askance . . .*

At the same time he agreed to the publication of his Autobiography in the Paris *L'Express*, where it began appearing serially on February 21. He was supposed to extend his tour and to visit Italy and the United States again. But within a short time, he was suddenly recalled to Moscow to face a barrage of official criticism and vituperation. The Autobiography had probably proved the last straw. It was far too uninhibited. But it has also been held that Yevtushenko's reading of "The Dead Hand" at the Mutualité in Paris had something to do with his recall. The point is that, as from March 8, when Mr. Khrushchev made a speech about the state of the Soviet arts, to the end of June, when the clamor began to die away, Yevtushenko, Voznesensky, and many other writers, young and old, were subjected to a veritable assault on their nerves. But there were no arrests or terror this time. It was expected that the writers would capitulate and make long speeches of apology and adapt themselves to the ideological requirements. Instead, after making a very brief and noncommital statement, Yevtushenko chose to ignore the whole matter and went off in May on a long trip to Zima Station and other parts of Siberia. He stayed for a time in a village at the mouth of the Pechora river, and by August he had completed a new cycle of poems. Part of the cycle was published in the September, 1963, issue of *Yunost*. This was a sign that the worst of the crisis was over. About six months had passed without Yevtushenko being published. But it is also true that the ideological "authorities," in the persons of L. Ilyichev and S. Pavlov, became disturbed by what they came to term "the conspiracy of silence," that is, the tacit refusal of notable writers like Ehrenburg and Paustovsky, Yevtushenko and Voznesensky, to take part in continuous public debates about the state of the arts and their relation to them. The writers had made their silent point and had managed to survive without anything too drastic happening to them.

Yevtushenko's poems in *Yunost* had been written between May and August. Besides "Again At Zima Station" and "People Were Laughing Behind A Wall," the cycle contains some lovely lyrical poems such as "Beautiful Are the Delights of Early Years," and also ballads such as "Olena's Feet." In this last the poet describes "Babushka Olena," a sturdy and self-sufficient old woman living in the wilds. At the end of the ballad, the poet implies that he, too, has sturdy legs and can stand on his own feet:

> *I'm not accustomed to stooping—*
> *I have preserved my pride,*
> *and sorrows will not*
> *knock me off my feet . . .*

In a number of these poems, as in "People Were Laughing," an intensification in Yevtushenko's lyrical mood can be detected:

> *People were laughing behind a wall.*
> *They seemed to be making fun of me.*
> *I was the butt of all their laughter,*
> *and how dishonestly they laughed.*

It was as if the Pechora air had made him breathe more deeply. In these poems he shows a greater command of poetical resources and seems to grow lyrically more powerful. It is also significant that many of the new poems are written in the ballad style which Yevtushenko handles very well. There is still a tradition of oral poetry extant in that part of the North where he had been staying. By contrast, he appears more superficial in "Again At Zima Station," an almost perfunctory description of his disgrace:

> *I have returned in no good standing,*
> *and after some sharp reprimands,*
> *which have their use in the final count . . .*

This *Yunost* cycle of poems was criticized in the December issue of *Oktyabr*, and Yevtushenko was again accused of "self-admiration," a charge often brought against him. However, on December 13, during Poetry Week, Yevtushenko did make a public appearance, and read a poem entitled "Ballad About the Punitive Battalion," in which he compared himself to a soldier in such a battalion.[7]

In 1964, Yevtushenko published more than in the preceding year —he had poems in the February *Moskva*, in *Literaturnaya Gazeta* of March 3, and in the July *Novy Mir*. There were nine poems in *Moskva*. Among them were "Nefertiti" and "Other Times Have Come," both poems with a polemical underlining, and "Wood-Cock" and "How Piaf Departed," two impressive lyrics. In March he published a longish poem, "The Execution of Stenka Razin," a few lines of which have already been quoted, and a strange long poem about Lenin and his relation to the Russian people. Both these poems are in the form of lyrical ballads. They are autonomous parts of a very long poem on which the poet had been working for the past year, a poem provisionally entitled "The Hydro-Power Station at Bratsk." This rather overpowering title cannot, however, give us any real idea of the poem. It will certainly *not* be anything like one of those Five Year Plan works of the early 1930's. The Stenka Razin part of it demonstrates that. "The Execution of Stenka Razin" is a strange poem or ballad, too. The theme is, of course, a defeated

---

7. During the war Punitive Battalions were under iron discipline and were given the most dangerous military tasks to perform, usually mine-clearing. They were made up of officers and men who had been convicted of military offenses.

rebel—a rebel who had expected to enter Moscow in triumph, but had instead been taken in a cart to the place of execution in Red Square. Yevtushenko's Stenka Razin has no regrets. He is only sorry he had not strung up more "boyars":

> I have sinned because,
> > though a foe of serfdom,
> I was yet part-serf myself.

This ballad breathes a note not only of bitterness and defeat, but also of resolution. One is naturally tempted to ask what connection the defeated rebel Stenka Razin has to Yevtushenko's own position. The first part of the finished "Bratsk" poem was supposed to have been printed in the January, 1965, issue of *Yunost*, but the magazine came out without it. This may be a matter of mere delay or something more significant. The next few months will no doubt tell.[8] But to go back to the July *Novy Mir* of 1964—it added six more Yevtushenko poems, including "Third Memory," "The Excavator," "On the Pechora," and "Beloved, Sleep," the latter a long love lyric with a sort of incantatory power about it. In the lyrical poem "Third Memory," as in "People Were Laughing," Yevtushenko conveys a poignant sense of isolation—an isolation which, it is true, he manages to overcome:

> We all live through an hour like this,
> when anguish sticks to you like glue
> and, in all nakedness exposed,
> all life appears devoid of meaning.

In "How Faltering You Are, My Speech," Yevtushenko concludes by comparing himself to the legendary Ivan-the-Fool:

> nipping into a cauldron of boiling pitch,
> to emerge therefrom a cocksure, brawny man,
> smiling confidently in a new caftan,
> and twitching his shoulder as if to say:
> "Well, would you like to test your strength!"

---

8. The "Bratsk" poem, a long cycle of lyrics and topical verses, finally appeared in the April "*Yunost*". In June–July, Yevtushenko was able to visit Italy and to appear briefly at the Spoleto Festival.

It can certainly be said that Yevtushenko, though he went through a period bordering on despair, has not faded away as a result of his "disgrace" and semi-incarceration. He is still resilient and energetic. His trip to Siberia has, in the end, apparently proved invigorating and stimulating if we are to judge by the quantity and quality of his later poems. There is a whole batch of them that has yet to be printed. He has grown poetically both in depth and breadth. The Yevtushenko of 1965 is certainly a much bigger, better, and more important poet than his namesake of 1959. As a disciple of Whitman, Mayakovsky, and Yesenin ("I feel kin to Yesenin / and Walt Whitman"), he can combine a more intimate lyricism with an ever-present urge to stretch out further and embrace a wide world of possibilities. There is every reason to suppose that he will continue to grow in stature. If at times he could only curb his facility and diminish his tendency to moralize, then he would become an even greater poet. But he would do so all the more rapidly if the tiresome, paternalistic restrictions were removed and if the following injunction in a poem of Bullat Okudzhava's is heeded:

> *Guard us poets from foolish hands,*
> *from stupid judgments, blind companions.*

Yevgeny Yevtushenko has been waging a battle for the freedom of poetry, for the liberty of expression, and if this has necessitated an emphatic statement here and there, it is his privilege. It remains to be seen if, as he himself wrote about his generation:

> *We're but the preface to a preface,*
> *a prologue to a newer prologue!*

New York, January 1965, October 1966   GEORGE REAVEY

By the middle of 1965 Yevtushenko had again made his appearance on the international scene. In the summer of 1965 and 1966 he attended the Spoleto Festival; in 1966 he went on a reading tour in Australia; in November-December of 1966 he came on his second visit to the United States, this time to read his poetry in New York, and other cities. In 1967 he attended a festival in Dakar, and in April and May spent some time in Spain, and in Portugal during the

Fatima celebrations. In the summer, he embarked upon a six-week trip down the long Siberian river Lena, but he was back in Moscow in time for Ilya Ehrenburg's funeral in September.

Yevtushenko's renewed trips abroad are an indication that in the past three years political pressure on and criticism of him have become less acute. By the summer of 1967 it was rather Andrey Voznesensky who found himself in trouble. After his American tour in April-May, 1967, Voznesensky, who had so far proved a poet of less obvious political implications, was barred from further travel abroad for the present.

Just as Yevtushenko's expedition down the Angara river in 1964 had resulted in his "Bratsk" cycle and poems treating of his impressions of people in the Russian Arctic, so his Lena trip has produced another cycle—"Verses from a Log." So far only a few of these poems have appeared in periodicals. These poems will no doubt also reflect the poet's preoccupation with the Russian earth, a variety of Russian characters, love for the Russian landscape, revolutionary ideals as opposed to bureaucratic cynicism. More than Voznesensky, more like Nekrasov, he has been concerned with Russian people and their fate. In his "Italian Tears," for example, he describes the treatment meted out under Stalin to a Russian war prisoner who is repatriated from Italy. His recent cycle "Italian Italy" includes poems such as "Heat in Rome" and "The Rhythms of Rome" in which the poet mingles gusto, affectionate interest, sharp observation, and flashes of irony.

In his latest volume *The Mail Boat* (1966), we also find such characteristic poems as "The Sigh" (intimate, lyrical, inward), "Fears" (optimistic social comment and condemnation of the Stalinist past—"Fears are dying out in Russia"), "Sleep, My Beloved" and "What Pain, My Love" (love lyrics), and "Cinderella" (lyrical, symbolic and civic). In "Cinderella" the poet reminds us that he has a civic duty to perform, that is, "to wash the dirty linen of the age." In another poem, "Impressions of the Western Cinema," Yevtushenko parodies the James Bond myth. Attuned to the shifting political atmosphere, he also makes a tentative anti-Mao sortie. In a later 1967 poem, "The Red Guards," he hits out at the Maoists more forcibly.

September 21, 1967   GEORGE REAVEY

I. Prologue

> *"Oh, those who are my generation!*
> *We're not the threshold, just a step.*
> *We're but the preface to a preface,*
> *a prologue to a newer prologue!"*

Пролог

Я разный,
        я натруженный
и праздный,
я целе
      и нецелесообразный,
я весь несовместимый,
                неудобный,
застенчивый и наглый,
злой и добрый.
Я так люблю,
        чтоб все перемежалось
и столько всякого во мне перемешалось:
от запада и до востока,
от зависти и до восторга.
Я знаю, вы мне скажете —
                где цельность?
Вот в этом всем огромная есть ценность!
Я вам необходим,
         я доверху завален,
как сеном молодым машина грузовая,
лечу сквозь голоса,
         сквозь ветки,
                свет и щебет,
и бабочки в глаза,
          и сено прет сквозь щели.
Да здравствуют движения! И жаркость,
и жадность, торжествующая жадность!

Границы мне мешают,
          мне неловко
не знать Буэнос-Айреса, Нью-Йорка,

I'm many-sided.
        I'm overworked,
and idle too.
I have a goal
        and yet I'm aimless.
I don't, all of me, fit in;
            I'm awkward,
shy and rude,
nasty and goodnatured.
I love it,
      when one thing follows another
and so much of everything is mixed in me:
from West to East,
from envy to delight.
I know, you'll ask:
        "What about the integral aim?"
There's tremendous value in this all!
I'm indispensable to you!
          I'm heaped as high
as a truck with fresh mown hay!
I fly through voices,
        through branches,
              light and chirping,
and butterflies flutter in my eyes,
           and hay pushes out of cracks.
I greet all movement! Ardour,
and eagerness, triumphant eagerness!

Frontiers are in my way.
        It is embarrassing
for me not to know Buenos Aires and New York.

хочу шататься, сколько надо,

                     Лондоном,

со всеми говорить,

                хотя б на ломаном,

мальчишкой,

          на автобусе повисшим,

хочу проехаться утренним Парижем.

Хочу искусства,

          разного, как я,

пусть мне искусство не дает житья

и обступает пусть

                 со всех сторон,

да я и так искусством осажден.

Я в самом разном сам собой увиден,

мне близки и Есенин,

                и Уитман,

и Мусоргским охваченная сцена,

и девственная линия Гогена.

Мне нравится

             и на коньках кататься,

И, черкая пером, не спать ночей,

мне нравится

            в лицо врагу смеяться,

и женщину нести через ручей.

Вгрызаюсь в книги

              и дрова таскаю,

грущу,

       чего-то смутного ищу.

I want to walk at will
                    through London,
and talk with everyone,
                    even in broken English.
I want to ride
            through Paris in the morning,
hanging on to a bus like a boy.
I want art to be
            as diverse as myself;
and what if art be my torment
and harass me
            on every side,
I am already by art besieged.

I've seen myself in every aspect:
I feel kin to Yesenin
                    and Walt Whitman,
to Moussorgsky grasping the whole stage,
and Gauguin's pure virgin line.

I like
        to use my skates in winter,
and, scribbling with a pen,
                        spend sleepless nights.
I like
        to defy an enemy to his face,
and bear a woman across a stream.

I bite into books, and carry firewood,
pine,
        seek something vague,

И алыми морозными кусками
арбуза августовского хрущу.

Пою и пью,
            не думая о смерти,
раскинув руки,
              падаю в траву,
и если я умру на белом свете,
то я умру от счастья, что живу.

and in the August heat I love to crunch
cool scarlet slices of watermelon.

I sing and drink,
                    giving no thought to death;
with arms outspread
                    I fall upon the grass,
and if, in this wide world, I come to die,
then I shall die from sheer joy of living.

1957.

II. Our Anxieties: Poems 1953–1959

*"And I reflected on the true and false,
the passage of the true into the false."*

М. Рощину

Я что-то часто замечаю,
к чьему-то, видно, торжеству,
что я рассыпанно мечтаю,
что я растрепанно живу.
Среди совсем нестрашных с виду
полужеланий,
                                получувств
щемит:
                неужто я не выйду,
неужто я не получусь?
Меня тревожит встреч напрасность,
что и ни сердцу, ни уму,
и та не праздничность,
                                                а праздность,
в моем гостящая дому,
и недоверье к многим книжкам,
и в настроеньях разнобой,
и подозрительное слишком
неупоение собой...

Со всем, чем раньше жил, порву я,
забуду разную беду,
на землю, теплую,
                                парную,
раскинув руки,
                                упаду.
О те, кто наше поколенье!
Мы лишь ступень, а не порог.
Мы лишь вступленье во вступленье,
к прологу новому пролог!

10

There's Something I Often Notice

TO M. ROSCHIN

There's something I often notice,
and someone apparently gloats over this,
that I'm rather scatter-brained,
and untidy in my way of living.
Among the, in appearance, harmless
half-desires
                    and half-feelings,
my pinching worry is:
                              I do all right?
What if I don't pull through?
I am disturbed by all the waste of meetings
that nourish neither heart nor mind,
by the sloth,
                    not the festive spirit,
that has taken lodging in my house;
by my mistrust for many books,
and the warring strains in all my moods,
and the far too suspect
non-enthusiasm for myself . . .

I'll break with all I lived with up to now,
forget my various mishaps,
with arms spread out
                              fall down
on the warm
                    and steamy earth.
Oh those who are my generation!
We're not the threshold, just a step.
We're but the preface to a preface,
a prologue to a newer prologue!

О мой ровесник,
                    друг мой верный!
Моя судьба —
                    в твоей судьбе.
Давай же будем откровенны
и скажем правду о себе.
Тревоги наши вместе сложим,
себе расскажем и другим,
какими быть уже не можем,
какими быть уже хотим.
Жалеть не будем об утрате,
самодовольство разлюбя.

Завязывается
                    характер
с тревоги первой за себя.

Oh you in years my equal,
                              my true friend!
My fate's
            contained in yours.
Then let us be extremely frank,
and speak the truth about ourselves.
Let us share our anxieties together,
discuss between us, tell others too,
what sort of men we can't be any longer,
what sort of men we now desire to be.
Fallen out of love with self-conceit,
we shall not regret the loss.

Character
            begins to form
at the first pinch of anxiety about ourselves.

1953.

Я шатаюсь в толкучке столичной
над веселой апрельской водой,
возмутительно нелогичный,
непростительно молодой.

Занимаю трамваи с бою,
увлеченно кому-то лгу,
и бегу я сам за собою,
и догнать себя не могу.

Удивляюсь баржам бокастым,
самолетам,
              стихам своим...
Наделили меня богатством.
Не сказали, что делать с ним.

Through the Crowded Streets

Through the crowded streets of the capital
I wander above the sprightly April waters,
revoltingly illogical,
inexcusably young.

I take tramcars by storm,
tell effervescent lies,
and run in my own footsteps
and can never catch up.

I'm astounded by the bulging barges,
the airplanes,
                  my own poems . . .
They've endowed me with wealth.
No one told me how to spend it.

1954.

Непримиримость

Все .силы даже прилагая,
признанья долго я прожду.
Я жизни дружбу предлагаю,
но предлагаю и вражду.
Не по-мещански сокрушаясь,
а у грядущего в долгу
со многим я не соглашаюсь
и согласиться не могу.
Пускай не раз придется круто,
и скажут:
«Лучше б помолчал...»
                    Хочу я ссориться по крупной
и не хочу
            по мелочам.
От силы собственной хмелею.
Смеюсь над спесью дутых слав.
И, чтобы стать еще сильнее,
я не скрываю, чем я слаб.
И для карьер не применимой
дорогой,
            обданной бедой,
иду,
      прямой,
                  непримиримый,
что означает —
                  молодой.

Irreconcilable

Even all my energies exerting,
I'll have to wait long for recognition.
I offer life my friendship,
and my hostility into the bargain.
Since I have no petty worries,
and am indebted to the future,
I disagree with a lot of things,
and cannot possibly agree with them.
It will go hard with me at times,
and they will say:
         "He'd better hold his tongue!"
I wish to quarrel in a big way,
not over trifles—
        such my wish.
My own strength intoxicates me.
I laugh at the arrogance of blown up reputations.
And to grow yet stronger,
I don't conceal my weakest spots.
And picking a road unsuited
for the making of a career,
        a road drenched with misfortune,
I stride on,
    plain-speaking,
        irreconcilable,
and that means—
    I am young.

1955.

Зависть

Завидую я.
              Этого секрета
не раскрывал я раньше никому.
Я знаю,
              что живет мальчишка где-то,
и очень я завидую ему.
Завидую тому,
              как он дерется, —
я не был так бесхитростен и смел.
Завидую тому,
              как он смеется, —
я так смеяться в детстве не умел.
Он вечно ходит в ссадинах и шишках —
я был всегда причесанней,
                                     целей.
Все те места,
              что пропускал я в книжках,
он не пропустит.
              Он и тут сильней.
Он будет честен жесткой прямотою,
злу не прощая за его добро,
и там, где я перо бросал: «Не стоит...» —
он скажет:
       «Стоит!» —
                   и возьмет перо.
Он, если не развяжет,
                          так разрубит,
где я ни развяжу,
              ни разрублю.

Envy

I envy.
        This secret
I have not revealed before.
I know
        there is somewhere a boy
whom I greatly envy.
I envy
        the way he fights;
I myself was never so guileless and bold.
I envy
        the way he laughs—
as a boy I could never laugh like that.
He always walks about with bumps and bruises;
I've always been better combed,
                        intact.
He will not miss
            all those passages in books
I've missed.
        Here he is stronger too.
He will be more blunt and harshly honest,
forgiving no evil even if it does some good;
and where I'd dropped my pen:
                "It isn't worth it . . ."
he'd assert:
        "It's worth it!"
                and pick up the pen.
If he can't unravel a knot,
           he'll cut it through,
where I can neither unravel a knot,
              nor cut it through.

Он, если уж полюбит,

                         не разлюбит,

а я и полюблю,

                да разлюблю.

Я скрою зависть.

                  Буду улыбаться.

Я притворюсь, как будто я простак:

«Кому-то же ведь надо улыбаться,

кому-то же ведь надо жить не так...»

Но сколько б ни внушал себе я это,

твердя:

             «Судьба у каждого своя...»,

мне не забыть, что есть мальчишка где-то,

что он добьется большего, чем я.

Once he falls in love,
                    he won't fall out of it,
while I keep falling in
                    and out of love.
I'll hide my envy.
                    Start to smile.
I'll pretend to be a simple soul:
"Someone has to smile;
someone has to live in a different way . . ."
But much as I tried to persuade myself of this,
repeating:
            "To each man his fate . . ."
I can't forget there is somewhere a boy
who will achieve far more than I.

1955 [1957–59–62].

С усмешкой о тебе иные судят:
«Ну кто же возражает —

                              даровит.

Но молод,

          молод.

                    Есть постарше люди.
Чего он все быстрее норовит?»
Качают головами,

              сожалея:
«Да, юность вечно —

                    что поделать с ней! —
казаться хочет лет своих взрослее...»
Ты слушай,

        а не слушайся.

                        Взрослей!
Таланту, а не возрасту будь равен.
Пусть разница смущает иногда.
Ты не страшись

            быть молодым, да ранним.
Быть молодым, да поздним —

                            вот беда!
Пусть у иных число усмешек множишь,
а ты взрослей —

                не бойся их смешить,
взрослей,

        пока взрослеть еще ты можешь,
спеши,

      покуда есть куда спешить.

Others May Judge You

Others may judge you with ironic smile:
"Well, who denies he's got

                          a gift?
But he's so young,
                  so very young.
                                There are older men about.
What's he after in such a hurry?"
Petulantly
          they shake their heads:
"Yes, youth eternally—
                      it can't be helped!—
tries to look older than its years . . ."
Listen to them,
               but take no heed.
                                Older!
Be equal to your talent, not your age.
At times let the gap between them be embarrassing.
Fear not
        to be young, precocious.
To be young and tardy—
                       that is wrong!
What if ironic smiles do multiply;
more mature—
            fear not to make them laugh;
more mature,
            while you still have time to grow,
make haste,
           while there's somewhere you can hurry.

1955.

Ты большая в любви.
                    Ты смелая.
Я же робок на каждом шагу.
Я плохого тебе не сделаю,
а хорошее вряд ли смогу.
Все мне кажется, будто бы по лесу
без тропинки ведешь меня ты.
Мы в дремучих цветах до пояса.
Не пойму я —
                    что за цветы.
Не годятся все прежние навыки.
Я не знаю,
            что делать и как.
Ты устала.
                    Ты просишься на руки.
Ты уже у меня на руках.
Перед нами все чистое,
                            раннее,
молодое,
            зовущее в путь.
Ты спокойна,
                и платье
                            дыханием
поднимает высокая грудь.
«Видишь,
            небо какое синее?
Слышишь,
птицы какие в лесу?
Ну так что же ты?
                    Ну?
                    Неси меня!»
А куда я тебя понесу?..

You Are Big in Love

You are big in love.
     And bold.
My every step is timid.
I'll cause you no harm,
and can hardly do you any good.
Seems you are leading me
off the beaten path through a forest.
Now we're up to our waist in wild flowers.
I don't even know
     what they are, these flowers.
My previous training is of no help here.
I'm uncertain
    what to do or how.
You're tired.
    You ask to be carried in my arms.
You are already in my arms.
Ahead of us stretches all that is pure,
       early,
young,
  and what bids us journey on.
How quiet you are!
    As you breathe,
      your high bosom
raises your dress.
"Do you see?
    What a blue sky!"
Can you tell
what birds sing in the forest?
Well, what are you waiting for?
     Well?
      Carry me then!"
And where shall I carry you?

Глубокий снег

По снегу белому на лыжах я бегу.
Бегу и думаю:
                            что в жизни я могу?
В себя гляжу,
            тужу,
                        припоминаю.
Что знаю я?
            Я ничего не знаю.
По снегу белому на лыжах я бегу.
В красивом городе есть площадь Ногина.
Она сейчас отсюда мне видна.
Там девушка живет одна.
                            Она
мне не жена.
                В меня не влюблена.
Чья в том вина?..
                        Ах, белое порханье!
Бегу.
    Мне и тревожно и легко.
Глубокий снег.
                Глубокое дыханье.
Над головою тоже глубоко.
Мне надо далеко...
Скрипите,
            лыжи милые,
                        скрипите,
а вы,
    далекая,
            забудьте про беду.
Скрепите сердце.
                Что-нибудь купите.

Deep Snow

I am skiing over the white snow.
Skiing fast, I ask:
                              "What can I do in life?"
I peer into myself,
                    strain,
                              remember.
What do I know?
                    I know nothing.
I am skiing over the white snow.
There's Nogin Square in the handsome town.
I can spy the square from where I am.
A girl I know lives there.
                              She
is no wife to me.
                    Nor is she in love.
Who is to blame? . . .
                    Ah, the white spume.
I am skiing fast.
                    I feel troubled and light.
The snow is deep.
                    And deep my breathing.
Overhead it's also deep.
It's a long way I have to go . . .
Creak on,
         dear skiis,
                    creak on,
and you,
         far away,
                    forget your distress.
Screw up your courage.
                    Go out and shop.

Спокойно спите.

        Я не пропаду.

Я закурить хочу.

        Ломаю спички.

От самого себя устал бежать.

Домой поеду.

        В жаркой электричке

кому-то буду лыжами мешать.

Приеду к девушке одной.

           Она все бросит.

Она венком большие косы носит.

Она скучала от меня вдали.

Она поцеловать себя попросит.

«Не подвели ли лыжи?» —

             тихо спросит.

«Нет, нет, — отвечу я, —

           не подвели...»

А сам задумаюсь.

        «Ты хочешь, милый, чаю?» —

«Нет». —

     «Что с тобой —

          понять я не могу...

Где ты сейчас?»

       Я головой качаю.

Что я отвечу?

      Я ей отвечаю:

«По снегу белому на лыжах я бегу».

Sleep soundly.
                    I'll not get lost.
I feel like smoking,
                    break some matches.
I'm weary of running from myself.
I'll ride home instead.
                    In a hot electric train
my skiis will jab some passenger.
Then I'll arrive and visit a girl.
                    She'll stop what she is doing.
She wears thick plaits in a garland.
She yearned for me from afar.
She will ask to be kissed.
"Did you have trouble with the skiis?"
                    She'll softly ask.
"No, no," I'll answer.
                    "No trouble at all" . . .
And I'll begin to think.
                    "A cup of tea, my dear?"
"No."
        "What's the matter?
                    I don't understand. . . .
Where are you now?"
                    I shake my head.
What shall I answer?
                    And I reply:
"I am skiing over the white snow."

1955.

Стихотворенье

        надел я на ветку.

Бьется оно,

      не дается ветру.

Просишь:

    — Сними его,

        не шути. —

Люди идут.

     Глядят с удивленьем.

Дерево

   машет

     стихотвореньем.

Спорить не надо.

     Надо идти.

— Ты ведь не помнишь его...

        — Это правда,

Но я напишу тебе новое завтра.

Стоит бояться таких пустяков!

Стихотворенье для ветки не тяжесть.

Я напишу тебе, сколько ты скажешь.

Сколько деревьев —

      столько стихов!

Как же с тобою дальше мы будем?

Может быть, это мы скоро забудем?

Нет,

   если плохо нам станет в пути,

вспомним,

     что где-то,

        полно озареньем,

I Hung a Poem on a Branch

I hung a poem
               on a branch.
Thrashing,
               it resists the wind.
"Take it down,
               don't joke,"
                      you urge.
People pass.
               Stare in surprise.
Here's a tree
          waving
               a poem.
Don't argue now.
               We have to go on.
"You don't know it by heart!" . . .
                      "That's true,
but I'll write a fresh poem for you tomorrow."
It's not worth being upset by such trifles!
A poem's not too heavy for a branch.
I'll write as many as you ask for,
as many poems
               as there are trees!
How shall we get on in the future together?
Perhaps, we shall soon forget this?
No,
     if we have trouble on the way,
we'll remember
               that somewhere,
                      bathed in light,

дерево
　　　машет
　　　　　стихотвореньем,
и улыбнемся:
　　　　　— Надо идти.

a tree
      is waving
              a poem,
and smiling we'll say:
                  " 'We have to go on'."...

1955.

Свадьбы

А. Межирову

О свадьбы в дни военные!
Обманчивый уют,
слова неоткровенные
о том, что не убьют...

Дорогой зимней, снежною,
сквозь ветер, бьющий зло,
лечу на свадьбу спешную
в соседнее село.
Походочкой расслабленной,
с челочкой на лбу
вхожу,
         плясун прославленный,
в гудящую избу.
Наряженный,
             взволнованный,
среди друзей,
             родных
сидит мобилизованный
растерянный жених.
Сидит с невестой Верою.
А через пару дней
шинель наденет серую,
на фронт поедет в ней.
Землей чужой,
             не местною
с винтовкою пойдет,
под пулею немецкою,
быть может, упадет.
В стакане брага пенная,
но пить ее невмочь.

34

Weddings

TO A. MEZHIROV

Weddings in days of war,
false cheating comfort,
those hollow phrases:
"He won't get killed . . ."

On a snowbound winter road,
slashed by a cruel wind,
I speed to a hasty wedding
in a neighboring village.
Gingerly I enter
a buzzing cottage,
I, a folk dancer of repute,
with a forelock dangling
                    from my forehead.
All spruced up,
              disturbed,
among relatives
              and friends
the bridegroom sits, just mobilized,
distraught.
Sits with Vera—his bride,
but in a day or two
he'll pull on a gray soldier's coat,
and, wearing it, leave for the front.
Then with a rifle
              he will go,
tramping over alien, not his local, soil;
a German bullet, perhaps,
will lay him low . . .
A glass of foaming mead,
but he hasn't the guts to drink.

Быть может, ночь их первая —
последняя их ночь.
Глядит он опечаленно
и болью всей души
мне через стол отчаянно:
«А ну, давай пляши!»

Забыли все о выпитом,
все смотрят на меня,
и вот иду я с вывертом,
подковами звеня.
То выдам дробь,
                        то по полу
носки проволоку́.
Свищу,
          в ладоши хлопаю,
взлетаю к потолку.
Летят по стенам лозунги,
что Гитлеру капут,
а у невесты
                        слезыньки
горючие
              текут.
Уже я измочаленный,
уже едва дышу...
«Пляши!..» —
                        кричат отчаянно,
и я опять пляшу...
Ступни как деревянные,
когда вернусь домой,

Their first night together
will likely be their last.
Chagrined, the bridegroom stares,
and with all his soul in anguish
cries to me across the table:
"Well, go on, why don't you dance!"

They all forget their drinking,
all fix me with goggling eyes,
and I slide and writhe,
beating a rhythm with my hooves.
Now I drum a tattoo,
                    now drag my toes
across the floor.
Whistling shrilly,
              I clap my hands,
leap up to near the ceiling.
Slogans on the wall fly past,
"Hitler will be kaput!"
But the bride
            scalds
her face
        with tears.
I'm already a wet rag,
barely catch my breath . . .
"Dance!"—
           they shout in desperation,
and I dance again . . .
Back home, my ankles
feel as stiff as wood;

но с новой свадьбы
                    пьяные
являются за мной.
Едва отпущен матерью,
на свадьбы вновь гляжу
и вновь у самой скатерти
вприсядочку хожу.
Невесте горько плачется,
стоят в слезах друзья.
Мне страшно.
            Мне не пляшется,
но не плясать —
            нельзя.

but from another wedding
                              drunken guests
come knocking at the door once more.
Soon as mother lets me go,
I'm off to weddings once again,
and round the tablecloth anew
I stamp my feet and bend my knees.
The bride sheds bitter tears,
friends are tearful too.
I'm full of fears.
                              My heart's not in the dance,
but it's impossible
                  not to go on dancing.

1955 [1957-59-62].

Он вернулся из долгого
отлученья от нас
и, затолканный толками,
пьет со мною сейчас.
Он отец мне по возрасту.
По призванию брат.
Невеселые волосы.
Пиджачок мешковат.
Вижу руки подробные,
все по ним узнаю,
и глаза исподбровные
смотрят в душу мою.
Нет покуда и комнаты,
и еда не жирна.
За жокея какого-то
замуж вышла жена.
Я об этом не спрашиваю.
Сам о женщине той
поминает со страшною,
неживой простотой.
Жадно слушает радио,
за печатью следит.
Все в нем дышит характером,
интересом гудит...
Пусть обида и лютая,
пусть ему не везло,
верит он в Революцию
убежденно и зло.
Я сижу растревоженный,
говорить не могу...

He Has Returned

He has returned to us
from a prolonged absence
and, jostled by arguments,
he's drinking with me at present.
In age he might be my father.
A brother by inclination.
His hair has lost its sparkle.
His jacket hangs like a sack.
His circumstantial hands
tell me everything,
and his sunken eyes
stare through my soul.
He has no lodging at present,
and he's rather short of food.
His wife went off and married
a jockey by profession.
I ask no questions.
He, himself, recalls
that woman with a bluntness
that's terrifying and deadly.
Greedily he listens to the radio,
and follows the daily press.
Every pore in him breathes character,
hums with interest . . .
Even though his was a cruel mishap,
even though he's had bad luck,
he still believes in the Revolution
with a fierce conviction.
I sit there deeply moved,
unable to say a word . . .

В черной курточке кожаной
он уходит в пургу.
И, не сбитый обидою,
я живу и борюсь.
Никому не завидую,
ничего не боюсь.

In his short black leather jacket,
he walks out into the blizzard.
And I live on and struggle,
not undone by hurt.
There's nobody I envy,
nothing that I fear.

1956.

Не понимаю,

               что со мною сталось?

Усталость, может, —

                      может, и усталость.

Расстраиваюсь быстро и грустнею,

когда краснеть бы нечего —

                           краснею.

А вот со мной недавно было в ГУМе,

да, в ГУМе,

               в мерном рокоте и гуле.

Там продавщица с завитками хилыми

руками неумелыми и милыми

мне шею обернула сантиметром.

Я раньше был не склонен к сантиментам,

а тут гляжу,

               и сердце болью сжалось,

и жалость,

          понимаете вы,

                     жалость

к ее усталым чистеньким рукам,

к халатику

          и хилым завиткам.

Вот книга...

        Я прочесть ее решаю!

Глава —

        ну так,

             обычная глава,

а не могу прочесть ее —

                   мешают

слезами заслоненные глаза.

Я все с собой на свете перепутал.

I Don't Understand

I don't understand
                what's come over me.
Perhaps I'm weary—
                  weary perhaps.
I'm so easily worried, upset,
and blush without cause
             to blush.
It was in the GUM not long ago it happened,
yes, in the GUM
            amid the steady din and grumbling.
A saleswoman with straggly curls,
with inept but darling hands,
measured the inches of my neck.
Not prone to sentiments before,
I now stared hard,
           and pain pinched my heart,
and pity,
     you must know,
              pure pity
felt for her clean, exhausted hands,
her smock
     and straggly curls.
Here's the book . . .
           I intend to read!
A chapter—
        just
           an ordinary chapter,
but I can't read—
         in a mist of tears
my eyes won't let me.
With myself I've confused all things.

Таюсь,

      боюсь искусства, как огня.

Виденья Малапаги,

                  Пера Гюнта,

мне кажется, —

                все это про меня.

А мне бубнят, и нету с этим сладу,

что я плохой,

              что с жизнью связан слабо.

Но если столько связано со мною,

я что-то значу, видимо,

                  и стою?

А если ничего собой не значу,

то отчего же

            мучаюсь и плачу?!

I retire into my shell,

                  fear art like fire.
The visions of Malapaga,

                  those of Peer Gynt,
seem, all of them, now

                  to apply to me.
But people insist, and I can't cope with it,
that I'm no good,

                  have so few ties with life.
But if I connect with so many things,
I must stand for something, apparently,

                  have some value?
And if I stand for nothing,
why then

                  do I suffer and weep?!

1956.

В. Бокову

Пахнет засолами,
пахнет молоком.
Ягоды засохлые
в сене молодом.
Я лежу, чего-то жду
каждою кровѝнкой,
в темном небе
                    звезду
шевелю травинкой.
Все забыл, все забыл,
будто напахался, —
с кем дружил,
                    кого любил,
над кем надсмехался.
В небе звездно и черно.
Ночь хорошая.
Я не знаю ничего,
ничегошеньки.
Баловали меня,
а я —
        как небалованный,
целовали меня,
а я —
        как нецелованный.

A Scent of Brine

TO V. BOKOV

A scent of brine,
a smell of milk;
and dried out berries
in the fresh-mown hay.
I lie there, waiting
in each drop of blood;
with a blade of grass
                    I stir
a star in the dark sky.
I've forgotten all, forgotten all,
as if I'd plowed all day:
my best friend,
                    my dearest love,
the butt of my sarcasms too.
The sky is full of stars and black,
A fine night it is.
But I know nothing,
not even a bit of anything.
They used to spoil me,
but I'm
        still unspoiled;
they used to kiss me,
but I'm
        still unkissed.

1956.

Концерт

На станции Зима, в гостях у дяди
стучал я на машинке, словно дятел,
а дядя мне: «Найти бы мне рецепт,
чтоб излечить тебя! Эх, парень глупый!
Пойдем-ка с нами в клуб. Сегодня в клубе
Иркутской филармонии концерт!

Все, все пойдем... У нас у всех билеты.
Гляди — помялись брюки у тебя...»
И вскоре шел я, смирный, приодетый,
в рубахе, теплой после утюга.

А по бокам, идя походкой важной,
за сапогами бережно следя,
одеколоном, водкою и ваксой
благоухали чинные дядья.

Был гвоздь программы — розовая туша
Антон Беспятных — русский богатырь.
Он делал все! Великолепно тужась,
зубами поднимал он связки гирь.

Он прыгал между острыми мечами,
на скрипке вальс изящно исполнял,
жонглировал бутылками, мячами
и элегантно на пол их ронял.

Платками сыпал он неутомимо,
связал в один их, развернул его,
а на платке был вышит голубь мира
идейным завершением всего.

The Concert

At *Zima* station, staying with my uncle,
I tapped like a woodpecker on my typewriter.
"If I could only find the right prescription
for you!" my uncle said. "Ekh, you silly fellow!
Let's to the club. There'll be a concert of
the Irkutsk Philharmonic at the club today!

All, all of us, will go . . . We all have tickets.
Just look, your trousers are so crumpled . . ."
Soon I was walking, docile, neatly dressed,
wearing a shirt still warm from the ironing.

And on each side, solemnly striding,
and watching after their boots with care,
sedately the uncles walked, scenting
of liquor, boot-polish, and cologne.

Anton Bespyatnikh topped the bill,
a hulk of pinky flesh, a Russian *bogatyr*.
He did all things! Straining magnificently,
he lifted bunches of weights with his teeth.

He did a sword-dance between sharp blades,
gracefully played a waltz on a fiddle,
juggled with bottles and many a ball,
and dropped them gracefully on the floor.

He whisked out handkerchiefs without number,
tied them all up in one, unfolded it, and there
embroidered was the dove of peace—
the ideological climax of it all.

А дяди хлопали: «Гляди-ка, ишь как ловко!
Ну и мастак, да ты взгляни, взгляни...»
И я — я тоже потихоньку хлопал,
иначе бы обиделись они.

Пошел один я, тих и незаметен,
Я думал о земле — я не витал.
Ну что концерт! Бог с ним, с концертом этим!
Да мало ли такого я видал!

Я столько видел трюков престарелых,
но с оформленьем новым, дорогим
и столько на подобных представленьях
не слишком, но подхлопывал другим.

Я столько видел росписей на ложках,
когда крупы на суп не наберешь...
И думал я о подлинном и ложном,
о переходе подлинного в ложь.

Давайте думать. Все мы виноваты
в досадности немалых мелочей —
в пустых стихах, в бесчисленных цитатах,
в стандартных окончаниях речей.

Я размышлял о многом. Есть два вида
любви. Одни своим любимым льстят.
Какой бы тяжкой ни была обида,
простят и даже думать не хотят.

The uncles clapped: "Look there, how smart!
A master, that's what he is! Just look . . ."
And I—I also clapped, though with restraint,
for otherwise they'd take offense.

Then I went off, inconspicuous and quiet.
I thought of earthly matters—no fantasies.
The concert! God be with it, with this concert!
I've witnessed plenty of such stuff.

I've seen so many ancient tricks
presented in a new, expensive form,
and often at performances like this
I have, with others, clapped a little.

I've seen so many painted wooden spoons
when we lacked buckwheat for the soup . . .
And I reflected on the true and false,
the passage of the true into the false.

Let us think. We're guilty, all of us,
of the vexation caused by largish trifles—
of hollow poems, unending quotations,
of speeches standardized in their conclusions.

I have reflected on many things. Love has
two aspects. Some flatter their beloved.
However grievous the hurt they suffer,
they will forgive, not even try to think.

Мы столько послевременной досады
хлебнули в дни недавние свои.
Нам не слепой любви к отчизне надо.
а думающей, пристальной любви.

Давайте думать о большом и малом,
чтоб жить глубоко, жить не как-нибудь.
Великое не может быть обманом,
но люди его могут обмануть.

Жить не хотим мы так, как ветер дунет.
Мы разберемся в наших почему.
Великое зовет. Давайте думать.
Давайте будем равными ему.

In recent days we have gulped down
so much that belatedly annoys us.
It's not blind love our country needs,
but love considerate and constant.

Let's ponder on things large and small,
how to live deeply, not just anyhow.
Nothing great can be imposture,
but people can impose upon it.

Not as the wind blows do we want to live.
We'll cope with our own questioning "Why?".
Greatness calls. Let us begin to think.
Let us prove equal to this greatness.

1956 [1962].

Поздравляю вас, мама,

с днем рождения вашего сына.

За него вы волнуетесь,

и волнуетесь сильно.

Вот лежит он,

худущий,

большой и неприбранный,

неразумно женатый,

для дома неприбыльный.

На него вы глядите

светло и туманно...

С днем рожденья

волнения вашего, мама!

Вы ему подарили

любовь беспощадную к веку,

в Революцию

трудную,

гордую веру.

Вы не дали ни славы ему,

ни богатства,

но зато подарили

талант не бояться.

Отворите же окна

в листву

и чириканье,

поцелуем

глаза его пробудите.

Подарите ему

тетрадь и чернильницу,

молоком напоите

и в путь проводите...

I Congratulate You, Mamma

I congratulate you, mamma,
                              on your son's birthday.
You worry about him,
                   and your worry is strong.
Here he lies,
           so gaunt,
                     large and untidy,
married unwisely,
                 unprofitable for the home.
You gaze on him
               with eyes bright and misted . . .
Congratulations, mamma,
                        on the birthday of your worry!
You have made him a present
                           of his ruthless love for this age,
a hard,
       proud faith
                    in the Revolution.
You gave him neither fame,
                          nor riches,
but you've given him instead
                            the ability not to fear.
Open the windows then
                     on the leaves
                                  and the warbling birds,
awake his eyes
              with a kiss.
Make him a present
                  of a notebook and inkstand,
give him his fill of milk
                         and speed him on his journey . . .

1956.   57

И. Глазунову

Когда я думаю о Блоке,
когда тоскую по нему,
то вспоминаю я не строки,
а мост, пролетку и Неву.
И над ночными голосами
чеканный облик седока —
круги под страшными глазами
и черный очерк сюртука.
Летят навстречу светы, тени,
дробятся звезды в мостовых,
и что-то выше, чем смятенье,
в сплетенье пальцев восковых.
И, как в загадочном прологе,
чья суть смутна и глубока,
в тумане тают стук пролетки,
булыжник, Блок и облака...

When I Think of Alexander Blok

TO I. GLAZUNOV

When I think of Alexander Blok,
and grow nostalgic for him,
I then remember—not some line of verse,
but a bridge, a carriage, and the Neva.
And above the voices in the night
a rider's figure is clearly etched—
the rings under his startling eyes,
and the outline of a black frockcoat.
Lights and shadows fly to meet him,
and stars in splinters fall on the roadways,
and the waxen fingers of his clasped hands
show something higher than dismay.
As in some very enigmatic prologue,
whose deep meaning is not too clear,
a mist envelops the rattling carriage,
the cobblestones, the clouds, and Blok . . .

1957.

Не знаю я,
                    чего он хочет,
но знаю —
                    он невдалеке.
Он где-то рядом,
                    рядом ходит
и держит яблоко в руке.
Пока я даром силы трачу,
он ходит,
        он не устает,
в билет обернутую сдачу
в троллейбусе передает.
Он смотрит,
            ловит каждый шорох,
Не упускает ничего,
не понимающий большого
предназначенья своего.
Все в мире ждет его,
                    желает,
о нем,
        неузнанном,
                    грустит,
а он по улицам гуляет
и крепким яблоком хрустит.
Но я робею перед мигом,
когда, поняв свои права,
он встанет,
            узнанный,
                    над миром
и скажет новые слова.

I Don't Know What He Wants

I don't know
               what he wants,
but I know
               he's not far off.
Somewhere near,
                  nearby he walks,
clutching an apple in his hand.
While I expend my strength in vain,
he walks about,
               untiring;
in a bus he passes on
change wrapped in a ticket.
He watches,
               catches the slightest sound,
misses nothing,
not understanding his own big
predestination.
Everything in the world awaits,
                              desires him,
yearns
     for him,
               the unrecognized,
but he just strolls about the streets,
crunching a firm apple.
But I quail before the instant
when, having understood his rights,
he'll rise up,
               now recognized,
                              above the world
and speak new words.
1957.

Карьера

Ю. Васильеву

Твердили пастыри, что вреден
и неразумен Галилей.
Но, как показывает время,
кто неразмуней — тот умней.

Ученый — сверстник Галилея
был Галилея не глупее.
Он знал, что вертится Земля,
но у него была семья.

И он, садясь с женой в карету,
свершив предательство свое,
считал, что делает карьеру,
а между тем губил ее.

За осознание планеты
шел Галилей один на риск,
и стал великим он... Вот это —
я понимаю — карьерист!

Итак, да здравствует карьера,
когда карьера такова,
как у Шекспира и Пастера,
Ньютона и Толстого... Льва!

Зачем их грязью покрывали?
Талант — талант, как ни клейми.
Забыты те, кто проклинали,
но помнят тех, кого кляли.

A Career

TO YU. VASILIEV

Galileo, the clergy maintained,
was a pernicious and stubborn man.
But time has a way of demonstrating
the most stubborn are the most intelligent.

In Galileo's day, a fellow scientist
was no more stupid than Galileo.
He was well aware the earth revolved,
but he also had a large family to feed.

Stepping into a carriage with his wife,
after effecting his betrayal,
he believed he was launched on a career,
though he was undermining it in reality.

Galileo alone had risked asserting
the truth about our planet,
and this made him a great man . . . His was
a genuine career as I understand it.

I salute then a career,
when the career is akin to
that of a Shakespeare or Pasteur,
a Newton or Tolstoy—Leo!

Why did people fling mud at them all?
Talent speaks for itself, whatever the charges.
We've forgotten the men who abused them,
Remember only the victims of slander.

Все те, кто рвались в стратосферу,
врачи, что гибли от холер,
вот эти делали карьеру!
Я с их карьер беру пример!

Я верю в их святую веру.
Их вера — мужество мое.
Я делаю себе карьеру
тем, что не делаю ее!

All who rushed into the stratosphere,
the doctors who perished fighting cholera,
were, all of them, men of career!
I take their careers as my example!

I believe in their sacred faith.
Their faith is my very manhood.
I shall therefore pursue my career
by trying not to pursue one.

1957.

Монолог из драмы «Ван-Гог»

Ю. Васильеву

Мы те,

   кто в дальнее уверовал, —
безденежные мастера.
Мы с вами из ребра Гомерова,
мы из Рембрандтова ребра.
Не надо нам

    ни света чопорного,
ни Магомета,

     ни Христа,
а надо только хлеба черного,
бумаги,

   глины

     и холста!
Смещайтесь, краски,

       знаки нотные!
По форме и земля стара —
мы придадим ей форму новую,
безденежные мастера!
Пусть слышим то свистки,

       то лаянье,
пусть дни превратности таят,
мы с вами отомстим талантливо
тем, кто не верит в наш талант!
Вперед,

  ломая

    и угадывая!
Вставайте, братья, —

      в путь пора.
Какие с вами мы богатые,
безденежные мастера!

Monologue from the Drama "Van Gogh"

TO YU. VASILIEV

We are the men
            who have believed in distant goals,
we the penniless masters.
We issued from Homer's rib,
from Rembrandt's rib.
We need
        no swollen-head society
neither Mahomet,
                nor Christ,
but only a crust of black bread,
paper,
      clay,
            and canvas!
Stir then, paints,
                and musical notes!
In form the earth is also old—
we shall endow her with a new form,
we the penniless masters!
What if we hear now catcalls,
                        now the baying pack,
what if the days are fraught with instability,
yet ably we shall be avenged
on those who disbelieve in our abilities!
Forward then,
            breaking fresh ground,
                            and guessing true!
Up, brothers,
            it's time to journey forth.
How rich we are,
we the penniless masters!

1957.

Моей собаке

В стекло уткнувши черный нос,
все ждет и ждет кого-то пес.

Я руку в шерсть его кладу,
и тоже я кого-то жду.

Ты помнишь, пес, пора была,
когда здесь женщина жила.

Но кто же мне была она —
не то сестра, не то жена,

а иногда, казалось, — дочь,
которой должен я помочь.

Она далеко... Ты притих.
Не будет женщин здесь других.

Мой славный пес, ты всем хорош,
и только жаль, что ты не пьешь!

To My Dog

With black muzzle pressed against a pane,
a dog keeps waiting, waiting.

I lay my hand upon its coat,
and also wait for someone to appear.

Do you remember, dog, there was a time
when a woman was living in this house?

But who was she to me?
A sister or a wife maybe,

and, at times, a daughter, too,
whom I felt obliged to help.

She's far away now . . . You're so quiet.
No other women will come here.

My dear old dog, you're good in every way,
but what a pity you don't drink.

1958.

Моя любимая приедет,
меня руками обоймет,
все изменения приметит,
все опасения поймет.
Из черных струй, из мглы кромешной,
забыв захлопнуть дверь такси,
взбежит по ветхому крылечку,
в жару от счастья и тоски.
Взбежит промокшая,

               без стука,
руками голову возьмет,
и шубка синяя со стула
счастливо на пол соскользнет...

My Beloved Will Arrive at Last

My beloved will arrive at last,
and fold me in her arms.
She will notice the least change in me,
and understand all my apprehensions.
Out of the black rain, the infernal gloom,
having forgotten to shut the taxi door,
she'll dash up the ricketty steps,
all flushed with joy and longing.
Drenched, she'll burst in

                without knocking,
and clasp my head in her hands;
and from a chair her blue fur coat
will slip blissfully to the floor . . .

1959.

Будем великими!

Э. Неизвестному

Требую с грузчика,
                    с доктора,
с того, кто мне шьет пальто, —
все надо делать здорово —
это неважно что!
Ничто не должно быть посредственно —
от зданий
            и до галош.
Посредственность неестественна,
как неестественна ложь.
Сами себе велите
славу свою добыть.

Стыдно не быть великим.
Каждый им должен быть!

72

Let Us Be Great

TO E. NEIZVESTNYI

I make demands of the trucker,
                          the doctor,
and the man who is making me an overcoat—
we must excell in everything,
no matter what!
There should be no mediocrity—
neither in buildings,
                          nor in galoshes.
Mediocrity is unnatural,
as unnatural as falsehood.
To win fame,
you must spur yourselves on.
Not to be great is shameful.
Everyone should be great!

1959.

Сердитые

Век двадцатый,
                    век великий спутника,
сколько в тебе скорбного и смутного,
ты — и добрый век,
                    и век-злодей,
век — убийца собственных идей,
век сердитых молодых людей.

Молодые люди сильно сердятся.
Их глаза презреньем к веку светятся.
Презирают партии,
                    правительства,
церковь
          и философов провидчества.
Презирают женщин,
                    спят с которыми,
землю с ее банками,
                    конторами.
Презирают
          в тягостном прозренье
собственное жалкое презренье.
Век двадцатый не отец им —
                    отчим.
Очень он не нравится им,
                    очень.
И броженье темное,
                    густое
в парнях ядовитых на Гудзоне;
и на Тибре,
          Сене
                    и на Темзе

The Angry Young Men

Twentieth century,
                    the great age of the sputnik,
you're so full of trouble and distress;
a generous age
                and evil too,
an age
      that murders your own ideas,
an age of angry young men.

The young men are extremely angry.
Their eyes shine with contempt for the age.
They despise political parties,
                                governments,
the church,
            and seers who philosophize.
They despise the women
                        with whom they sleep,
the world of Banks
                  and offices.
They despise
            with painful insight
their own sorry contempt.
The twentieth century is no father to them—
                                    only a stepfather.
They greatly dislike it,
                        greatly.
And a dark,
          dense ferment
seizes on the caustic fellows by the Hudson;
and by the Tiber,
                  the Seine,
                            and the Thames,

парни ходят сумрачные те же.
Резкие,
            угрюмые,
                        неладные,
веку они вроде ни к чему...
Понимаю я —
                чего не надо им.
А чего им надо —
                    не пойму.
Неужели юности их кредо
только в том,
                чтоб выругаться крепко?!
Я сейчас отсюда,
                из Москвы,
говорю им просто,
                    по-мужски:
если я на что-то и сердит,
это оттого лишь, что во мне
не безверье жалкое сидит,
а гудит любовь к родной стране.
Если я на что-то и сержусь —
это оттого, что я горжусь
тем, что я с друзьями,
                        я в строю,
я в бою
        за правоту мою!
Что там с вами?
                    Ищете ли правды?
«Массовый психоз», —
                    вздыхают медики.

the same frowning fellows wander.
Curt,
      surly,
               uneasy,
they seem outsiders to the age . . .
I can understand
                    what they don't want.
But what they want,
                       that I don't understand.
Surely their youthful credo
is not just their capacity
                     to swear like hell?!
At this moment here,
                from Moscow,
I speak to them bluntly,
                  man to man:
If I'm moved to anger,
it's not because I harbor
wretched disbelief—
but because I'm loud in my love for my country.
If I'm moved to anger,
it is because I'm proud
to be with friends,
               in the ranks,
battling
      for my right!
What's the matter with you there?
                    Do you seek truth?
"Mass psychosis,"
          sigh the psychiatrists.

По Европе мрачно бродят парни.
Мрачно бродят парни по Америке.
Век двадцатый,

            век великий спутника,
вырви их из темного и спутанного!
Дай им не спокойствие удобное —
дай им веру

            в праведное,

                        доброе.
Это дети,

        это не враги.
Век двадцатый —

            слышишь? —

                    помоги!

Brooding fellows wander all over Europe.
Broodingly they wander all over America.
Twentieth century,
                        the great age of the sputnik,
pluck them out of their dark confusion.
Grant them no convenient quietude.
Grant them faith
                in what's righteous
                                and beneficent.
They are children,
                —not enemies.
Twentieth century—
                do you hear?—
                                help us!

1959 [1962].

У трусов малые возможности.
Молчаньем славы не добыть,
и смелыми
из осторожности
подчас приходится им быть.
И лезут в соколы ужи,
сменив с учетом современности
приспособленчество ко лжи
приспособленчеством ко смелости.

Cowards Have Small Possibilities

Cowards have small possibilities.
Fame is not won through silence,
and cowards,
            out of caution,
are at times obliged to show courage.
Thus adders hustle to be hawks;
sensing the way the wind is blowing,
they adapt themselves to courage
just as they had adapted themselves to lies.

1959.

III. A Conversation with an American Writer: Poems 1960–1962

"Poetry
          is no chapel of peace.
     Poetry is savage war."

Свежести!
        Свежести!
Хочется свежести!
Свадебной снежности
и незаслеженности,
свежести мускулов,
мозга,
        мазка,
свежести музыки
и языка!
Чтоб не держалось,
а провалилось
все, что слежалось
и пропылилось.
Чтоб с неизбежностью
просто
        и быстро
свержено
        свежестью
все это было.
Много ли проку
в том,
        как возятся
те,
    кто против
свежего воздуха?
Кем это сдержится?
Это не сдержится!
Свежести!
        Свежести!
Хочется свежести!

Freshness

Freshness!
        Freshness!
We want freshness!
Pure nuptial snow,
and no tracks,
freshness of muscle,
brain,
      brush stroke,
freshness in music
and language!
May all things long-lain,
crusted with dust,
crumble away,
and not stay there stale.
May freshness
with all inevitability
very simply
        and quickly
displace
      all this.
What's the use
their making
        a fuss—
those
    who object
to fresh air?
Who will maintain it?
It won't be sustained!
Freshness!
        Freshness!
We want freshness!

1960.

Когда взошло твое лицо
над жизнью скомканной моею,
вначале понял я лишь то,
как скудно все, что я имею.
Но рощи, реки и моря
оно особо осветило
и в краски мира посвятило
непосвященного меня.
Я так боюсь, я так боюсь
конца нежданного восхода,
конца открытий, слез, восторга,
но с этим страхом не борюсь.
Я понимаю — этот страх
и есть любовь. Его лелею,
хотя лелеять не умею,
своей любви небрежный страж.
Я страхом этим взят в кольцо.
Мгновенья эти — знаю — кратки,
и для меня исчезнут краски,
когда зайдет твое лицо...

When Your Face Came Rising

When your face came rising
above my crumpled life,
the only thing I understood at first
was how meager were all my possessions.
But your face cast a peculiar glow
on forests, seas, and rivers,
initiating into the colors of the world
uninitiated me.
I'm so afraid, I'm so afraid,
the unexpected dawn might end,
ending the discoveries, tears, and raptures,
but I refuse to fight this fear.
This fear—I understand—
is love itself. I cherish this fear,
not knowing how to cherish,
I, careless guardian of my love.
This fear has ringed me tightly.
These moments are so brief, I know,
and, for me, the colors will disappear
when once your face has set . . .

1960.

Ракеты и телеги

Телегу обижать не надо.
Телега сделала свое.
Но часто,
                    будь она неладна,
в искусстве вижу я ее.
Гляжу я с грустью на коллегу
и на его роман-
                    телегу.
Мы лунник в небо запустили,
а оперы —
                    в тележном стиле.
О дух дегтярный,
                    дух рутины!
Ведь есть телеги —
                            не картины.
И, грохоча, как бы таран,
телеги лезут на экран.
О вы, кто так телегам рады, —
у вас тележный интеллект.
Вам не ракет в искусстве надо —
телег вам надобно,
                    телег.
Искусство ваше и прилежно,
и в звания облачено,
но все равно оно
                    тележно
и в век ракет
                    обречено!

Rockets and Carts

We should not sniff at carts.
The cart has done good service.
But how often,
                    though hardly fitting now,
I still perceive the cart in art.
How depressing to stare at a colleague
and at his cart-
                    the-novel.
We've already shot a lunic into the sky,
but our operas
                    still retain a cart-like style.
O cart-grease spirit!
                    Spirit of routine!
Carts do exist—
                    no pictures.
And yet rumbling like a battering ram,
carts push their way on to the screen.
O you who are so pleased with carts,
what a cart-like mind you own.
You want no rockets in your art;
it's carts you want,
                    just carts.
Your art's most diligent,
wrapped in the label of "vocation";
but all the same
                    it's like a cart,
and in an age of rockets
                    doomed.

1960.

Москва-Товарная

М. Павлову

Студенту хочется

                    послушать Скрябина,

и вот полмесяца

                    живет он скрягою.

Ему не падает

           с неба манна.

Идей до черта,

              а денег мало!

Судьба коварная

                  под корень рубит,

но, проявляя, как мать, заботу,

Москва-Товарная

                 студентов любит

и выручает —

           дает работу.

Ночь над перроном идет на убыль.

Сгружают медики под песни уголь.

Сгружают лирики,

                сгружают физики

дрова и сахар,

             цемент и финики.

Состав с арбузами

                пришел из Астрахани!

Его встречают

           чуть ли не с астрами!

Студенты —

        грузчики

              такие страстные!

Летают в воздухе

             арбузы страшные,

Moscow Freight Station

TO M. PAVLOV

A student wants
                    to sit listening to Scriabin,
and for the last six months
                        he's been living hand to mouth.
For him manna
                does not fall from heaven.
A devil of a lot of ideas,
                            but hardly any money!
Insidious fate
                hacks at the roots,
but, showing a mother's solicitude,
the Moscow Freight Station
                                loves students
and gives them a helping hand—
                            gives them work.

The night fades above the railroad platform.
Meds sing, unloading coal.
Lyricists unload,
                    physicists unload,
logs of wood and sugar,
                        cement and figs.
A freight of watermelons
                        pulls in from Astrakhan!
They almost greet it
                    with bouquets of asters!
The students
            are such passionate handlers!
Through the air they fly,
                        these terrifying watermelons,

и с уважением

        глядит милиция

и на мэитовца,

          и на миитовца.

Но вот светает.

        Конец разгрузу.

Всем по двадцатке

        и по арбузу.

В карман двадцатку,

         и к кассе — в полдень.

Теперь со Скрябиным

         порядок полный.

Арбузы просто первый сорт —

          спасибо Астрахани!

Сидят студенты на перроне,

          громко завтракают

и поездам,

так и мелькающим над шпалами,

с перрона машут

         полумесяцами алыми...

А столько свежести

         и молодости в воздухе!

И под арбузы,

        под гудки паровозные

у них дискуссии и тут

         во всем размахе

о кибернетике,

      о Марсе,

        о Ремарке.

and the militiamen stare
                    with respect
at both the engineering
                    and the transport students.
But it grows light.
                    They've finished unloading.
They each get twenty rubles
                    and a melon.
They pocket their twenty
                    and will storm the box office at noon.
Now everything is all right
                    with Scriabin.
The watermelons are first class—
                    thanks to Astrakhan!
Now the students sit on the platform,
                    loudly breakfasting,
and from the platform
                    they wave scarlet half-moons
at the trains
                    that keep gliding over the ties.
How much freshness
                    and youth is in the air!
Munching watermelons,
                    as the locomotives hoot,
they plunge into arguments even here
                    full swing
about cybernetics,
                    Mars,
                    and Remarque.

Москва-Товарная,

            запомни их, пожалуйста, —

ну где им равные

               по силе

                    и по жадности!

Они приходят

            из Рязаней,

                 из Вологд.

Они ночей не спят —

                  бумагу изводят,

но, пусть придется долго им помучиться,

из них,

       настырных,

                  добрый толк получится!

Им предстоят открытья величайшие.

От них зависеть будут судьбы мира.

Ну а пока —

             за то, что выручаешь их,

Москва-Товарная,

             спасибо тебе, милая!

Moscow Freight Station,
                    remember them please—
where else would you find
                    their equals in strength
                              and fervor.
They come from places like Ryazan,
                    like Vologda.
They don't sleep nights—
                    devouring paper,
but if they stick it long enough,
they'll make good material,
                    these boys,
                              who've roughed it.
The greatest discoveries await them.
On them the world's destinies will depend.
But in the meantime—
                    because of your assistance,
Moscow Freight Station,
                    many thanks to you, my dear!

1960.

Юмор

Цари,
      короли,
            императоры,
властители всей земли,
командовали парадами,
но юмором —

                  не могли.
В дворцы именитых особ,
все дни возлежащих выхоленно,
являлся бродяга — Эзоп,
и нищими они выглядели.
В домах,
      где ханжа наследил
своими ногами щуплыми,
всю пошлость
            Ходжа Насреддин
сшибал,
      как шахматы,
                  шутками!
Хотели
      юмор
            купить —
да только его не купишь!
Хотели
      юмор
            убить,
а юмор
      показывал
                  кукиш!
Бороться с ним —
            дело трудное.

Humor

Tsars,
      Kings,
            Emperors,
sovereigns of all the earth,
have commanded many a parade,
but they could not command
                  humor.
When Aesop, the tramp, came visiting
the palaces of eminent personages
ensconced in sleek comfort all day,
they struck him as paupers.
In houses,
        where hypocrites have
left the smear of their puny feet,
there Hodja-Nasr-ed-Din,
               with his jests,
swept clean
        all meanness
            like a board of chessmen!
They tried
        to commission
            humor—
but humor is not to be bought!
They tried
        to murder
           humor,
but humor
        thumbed
           his nose at them!
It's hard
        to fight humor.

Казнили его без конца.
Его голова отрубленная
торчала на пике стрельца.
Но лишь скоморошьи дудочки
свой начинали сказ,
он звонко кричал:

               «Я туточки!» —
и лихо пускался в пляс.
В потрепанном куцем пальтишке,
понурясь

         и вроде каясь,
преступником политическим
он,

      пойманный,

               шел на казнь.
Всем видом покорность выказывал,
готов к неземному житью,
как вдруг

        из пальтишка

             выскальзывал,
рукою махал

         и — тю-тю!
Юмор

     прятали

         в камеры,
но черта с два удалось.
Решетки и стены каменные
он проходил насквозь.
Откашлявшись простуженно,
как рядовой боец,

They executed him time and again.
His hacked-off head
was stuck on the point of a pike.
But as soon as the mummers' pipes
began their quipping tale,
humor defiantly cried:

                "I'm back, I'm here!",
and started to foot a dance.
In an overcoat, shabby and short,
with eyes cast down

              and a mask of repentence,
he,
    a political criminal,
now under arrest,

             walked to his execution.
He appeared to submit in every way,
accepting the life-beyond,
but of a sudden

          he wriggled out

                  of his coat,
and, waving his hand,

             did a bolt.
Humor
     was shoved

          into cells,
but much good that did.
Humor went straight through
prison bars and walls of stone.
Coughing from the lungs
like any man in the ranks,

шагал он

       частушкой-простушкой

с винтовкой на Зимний дворец.

Привык он ко взглядам сумрачным,

но это ему не вредит,

и сам на себя

           с юмором

юмор порой глядит.

Он вечен.

      Он, ловок и юрок,

пройдет через всё,

           через всех.

Итак —

     да славится юмор.

Он —

     мужественный человек.

he marched
            singing a popular ditty,
rifle in hand upon the Winter Palace.
He's accustomed to frowning looks,
but they do him no harm;
and humor at times
                    with humor
glances at himself.
He's everpresent.
                Nimble and quick,
he'll slip through anything,
                        through everyone.
So—
    glory be to humor.
He—
    is a valiant man.

1960.

Петухи

Т. Чиладзе

Кричат у моря петухи,
бряцая крыльями над Крымом.
Они кричат — и этим криком
дач сотрясают потолки.
Они велят шуметь и цвесть
и всё для этой цели будят,
они зовут к тому, что будет,
благословляя то, что есть.

Что есть, что будет у меня?
Не знаю этого детально,
но для меня одно не тайна
в начале и на склоне дня.
Среди неглавных мук и ласк
ты — ласка главная и мука,
моя измученная муза,
с кругами темными у глаз.
Любим ли я тобой? Любим,
но как-то горько и печально.
Ты смотришь на меня прощально,
как будто стал совсем другим.

Я изменяю, не любя,
тебе с подобьями твоими.
Твое приписываю имя
так не похожим на тебя.
Но, с болью видя эту ложь,
без громких слез, без нареканий,
коленки обхватив руками,
меня, как девочка, ты ждешь.
Как обратить твое «прощай»

The Cocks

TO T. CHILADZE

The cocks are crowing by the sea,
brandishing their wings over the Crimea.
They crow—and with their screeching
shake the cottage ceilings.
They bid us be loud, robust, and flourish,
and to this end they keep on waking us.
They summon us to what is in the future,
blessing what is now already here.

What have I? And what shall I have?
This I do not know in detail,
but there's one thing I find no mystery
at sunrise or at the close of day.
Amid the trivial torments and delights,
it is you—my tortured Muse,
with those dark rings under your eyes,
who are my torment and delight in chief.
Am I beloved of you? Beloved, yes,
but somehow with bitterness and grief.
You gaze at me with eyes of sad farewell,
as if I had changed beyond recall.

Unloving, I go on betraying you
with what are mere semblances of yourself.
Your name I frequently ascribe
to those so utterly unlike you.
But detecting this lie that hurts,
you shed no noisy tears, fling no reproaches,
and clasping your frail knees, continue
waiting for me like a little girl.
How can I transform your sad "farewell"

в простое утреннее «здравствуй»?
Будь не застенчивой, а властной,
и требуй, а не вопрошай!
Пускай измен моих не счесть,
пускай меня с усмешкой судят,
ты для меня и то, что будет,
ты для меня и то, что есть!

Кричат у моря петухи,
велят вставать и одеваться.
Они зовут не поддаваться,
оставив трусам поддавки.
Сигналы вечные вокруг.
Они зовут ко взрыву сонности,
будь это сонность нашей совести
иль сонность разума и рук.

Спасибо, жизнь, за трудный труд,
за петухов твоих упрямых!
Куда б себя я ни упрятал,
они найдут меня, найдут!
Благодарю тебя за сны,
благодарю за пробужденья,
за горькие предупрежденья,
что были мне тобой даны.
За столько всяческих грехов
и все же — за твою безгрешность,
за море, за его безбрежность
и еще раз — за петухов!

into a greeting as simple as "good morning"?
Do not be timid; be commanding,
make demands instead of pleading!
Though my betrayals cannot be numbered,
and I be judged with an ironic smile,
for me, you are the image of the future,
and also what is now already here.

The cocks are crowing by the sea,
commanding us to rise and dress.
They summon us to stop from yielding,
leaving it to cowards to "play at losing".
Eternal signals ring us round.
They summon us to shatter sleep,
be it the drowsiness of our conscience,
or the drowsiness of our reason and our hands.

Thank you, life, for the laborious labor,
for your cocks so stubborn ever!
They will find me, find me, I am certain,
wherever I may happen to be skulking!
Thank you also for the many dreams,
and thank you, too, for the awakening,
for all the bitter warnings
you have given me.
For such a multitude of every sin,
and also for your sinlessness,
for the sea and for its boundlessness,
and for your crowing cocks again.

1960, *Koktebel*.

Уходят матери

Р. Поспелову

Уходят наши матери от нас,
уходят потихонечку,
                        на цыпочках,
а мы спокойно спим,
                        едой насытившись,
не замечая этот страшный час.
Уходят матери от нас не сразу,
                              нет —
нам это только кажется, что сразу.
Они уходят медленно и странно
шагами маленькими по ступеням лет.
Вдруг спохватившись нервно в кой-то год,
им отмечаем шумно дни рожденья,
но это запоздалое раденье
ни их,
        ни наши души не спасет.
Все удаляются они,
                    все удаляются.
К ним тянемся,
                очнувшись ото сна,
но руки вдруг о воздух ударяются —
в нем выросла стеклянная стена!
Мы опоздали.
                Пробил страшный час.
Глядим мы со слезами потаенными,
как тихими суровыми колоннами
уходят наши матери от нас...

Our Mothers Depart

TO R. POSPELOV

Our mothers depart from us,
gently depart
                    on tiptoe,
but we sleep soundly,
                         stuffed with food,
and fail to notice this dread hour.
Our mothers do not leave us suddenly,

                              no—
it only seems so "sudden".
Slowly they depart, and strangely,
with short steps down the stairs of years.
One year, remembering nervously,
we make a fuss to mark their birthday,
but this belated zeal
will save neither their souls

                         nor ours.
They withdraw ever further,
                              withdraw ever further.
Roused from sleep,
                    we stretch toward them,
but our hands suddenly beat the air—
a wall of glass has grown up there!
We were too late.
                    The dread hour had struck.
Suppressing tears, we watch our mothers,
in columns quiet and austere,
departing from us . . .

1960.

Я жил многожеланно
и чуть-чуть курьезно:
все —
           то слишком рано
или —
           слишком поздно!
Жадно в жизнь вцеплялся,
душу раздроблял.
Рано я влюблялся,
рано разлюблял.
Не поступал я подло,
не поступлю и впредь,
но поздно начал,
                    поздно
я людей жалеть.

Все кончено,
           все кончено...
А было ли что начато?
И нытика
          не корчил я,
а начинал
           все начерно.
И вот стою над Волгою
посреди Руси
не хилый,
          не надорванный, —
что хошь на горб грузи!

Дышит влажной свежестью
звездная вода.

I Lived with Many Desires

I lived with many desires
and a little strangely too:
everything
            was either too early
or
    much too late!
Greedily I clutched at life,
split my soul in pieces.
I fell early in love,
and early out of love.
I didn't act meanly,
nor shall I do so in the future,
but late I had begun,
                    very late,
to have compassion for people.

All's ended,
            all's ended. . .
But was anything ever begun?
I never played
            the grumbler,
I started everything
                from scratch.
And now I stand over the Volga,
in the middle of Russia,
no weakling,
            no broken down man—
pile as much as you wish on my hump!

The starlit waters
breathe moist and fresh.

Пароходы светятся,
будто города.
Мне совсем не странно,
что настолько звездно,
и ничто не рано,
и ничто не поздно!

The steamers glow
like cities.
I'm not surprised
to see so many stars,
and nothing is early,
and nothing late!

1960.

Встреча в Копенгагене

Мы на аэродроме в Копенгагене
сидели и на кофе налегали.
Там было все изящно,
                              комфортабельно
и до изнеможенья элегантно.
И вдруг он появился —
                              тот старик —
в простой зеленой куртке с капюшоном,
с лицом,
              соленым ветром обожженным,
верней,
              не появился,
                              а возник.
Он шел,
              толпу туристов бороздя,
как будто только-только от штурвала,
и, как морская пена,
                              борода
его лицо,
              белея,
                              окаймляла.
С решимостью угрюмою победною
он шел,
              рождая крупную волну,
сквозь старину,
                              что под модерн подделана,
сквозь всяческий модерн под старину.
И, распахнув рубахи грубый ворот,
он, отвергая вермут и перно,
спросил у стойки рюмку русской водки,
и соду он отвел рукою:

A Meeting in Copenhagen

We are sitting at an airport
in Copenhagen drinking a lot of coffee.
It was most elegant there,
                    and comfortable,
and refined to the point of lassitude.
Then suddenly he appeared—
                      that old man—
in a plain green parka with a hood,
his face
        deep tanned by salt and wind—
loomed up
         rather
            than appeared.
He walked,
        furrowing through a crowd of tourists,
as if he'd just been sailing a boat,
and like the sea foam
            his beard,
whitening it,
         fringed
           his face.
With grim victorious determination
he walked,
        generating a big wave,
that swept through the modernized
                antique,
through every sort of antiqued modernity.
And pulling open the coarse collar of his shirt,
he, rejecting a vermouth and a pernod,
ordered a glass of Russian vodka at the bar
and pushed back the tonic with his hand:

«No...»

С дублеными руками в шрамах,

                            ссадинах,
в ботинках, издававших тяжкий стук,
в штанах, неописуемо засаленных,
он элегантней был,

                   чем все вокруг!
Земля под ним, казалось, прогибалась —
так он шагал увесисто по ней.
И кто-то наш сказал мне, улыбаясь:
«Смотри-ка,

            прямо как Хемингуэй!»
Он шел, в коротком жесте каждом

                              выраженный,
тяжелою походкой рыбака,
весь из скалы гранитной грубо вырубленный,
шел, как идут сквозь пули,

                          сквозь века.
Он шел, пригнувшись, будто бы в траншее,
шел, раздвигая стулья и людей...
Он так похож был

                 на Хемингуэя!
...А после я узнал,

                   что это был Хемингуэй.

"No!"

With rough-hewn hands, all scarred

and dented,

in boots that made a mighty clatter,
in trousers indescribably stained and greasy,
he looked more spruce

than anything nearby.

The earth seemed to bend beneath him—
so heavily did he tread upon it.
And one of us said to me with a smile:
"Just look!

The very spit of Hemingway!"
Expressed in each brief gesture,

he strode off

with a fisherman's ponderous gait,
all out of granite crudely hewn,
strode as men stride through gunfire,

through the ages,

He strode as if stooping in a trench;
strode shoving chairs and men aside . . .
He resembled

Hemingway so much!
Later I learned

it was, indeed, Hemingway!

April, 1960.

Американский соловей

В стране перлона и дакрона
и ставших фетишем наук
я вдруг услышал кровный-кровный
неповторимо чистый звук.
Для ветки птица — не нагрузка,
и на одной из тех ветвей
сидел и пел он, словно русский,
американский соловей.
Он пел печально и счастливо,
и кто-то, буйствуя, исторг
ему в ответ сирени взрывы —
земли проснувшийся восторг.
То было в Гарварде весеннем.
В нем все летело кверху дном —
в смеющемся и карусельном,
послеэкзаменно хмельном.
Студенты пели и кутили,
и все, казалось, до основ
смешалось в радужном коктейле
из птиц, студентов и цветов.
Гремел он гордо, непреложно,
тот соловей, такой родной,
над полуправдою и ложью,
над суетливой говорней,
над всеми черными делами,
над миллионами анкет
и над акульими телами
готовых к действию ракет.
А где-то в глубине российской
такой же маленький пострел,
свой клювик празднично раскрывший,

The American Nightingale

In the land of perlon and dacron,
and of science that has become a fetish,
I suddenly heard a kindred, kindred sound —
a sound quite inimitable and pure.
A branch can easily bear a bird,
and on one of those branches
this American nightingale was perched,
singing just like a Russian nightingale.
Mournfully he sang, and happily,
and someone stormily unleashed
flashes of lilac clusters in reply—
this earth's awakening joy.
This was in Harvard in the spring.
There everything was topsy-turvy—
in laughing Harvard's merry-go-round,
swaying drunkenly after the exams.
The students sang, out on a spree,
and to their foundations all things
seemed mixed in a rainbow cocktail
of students, birds, and flowers.
Proudly, unfailingly, that nightingale—
that so kindred nightingale—thundered
above the half-truths and the lies,
above all the restless chatter,
above all the black deeds,
above the millions of questionnaires
and the shark-like bodies
waiting for rockets to spring into action.
And somewhere in the heart of Russia
the same sort of little scamp,
festively opening his small beak,

его братишка русский пел.
В Тамбове, Гарварде, Майами
на радость сел и городов
под наливными соловьями
сгибались ветви всех садов.
Хлестала музыка, как вьюга,
с материка на материк...
Все соловьи поймут друг друга.
У них везде один язык.
Поют все тоньше, все нежнее
в единстве трепетном своем...
А мы-то, люди, неужели
друг друга так и не поймем?!

С Ш А ,   Г а р в а р д

his little Russian brother sang.
In Tambov, Harvard, and Miami,
for the delight of villages and cities,
the branches in all the gardens bent
beneath the nightingales in ecstasy.
The music, like a blizzard, lashed
one continent and then another . . .
All nightingales will understand each other;
everywhere they speak one language.
In their tremulous union,
they sing ever higher, more tenderly.
But we men, shall we never
understand each other?!

Harvard, U.S.A., 1961 [1962].

Битница

Эта девочка из Нью-Йорка,
но ему не принадлежит.
Эта девочка вдоль неона
от самой же себя бежит.

Этой девочке ненавистен
мир — освистанный моралист.
Для нее не осталось в нем истин.
Заменяет ей истины «твист».

И с нечесаными волосами,
в грубом свитере и очках
пляшет худенькое отрицанье
на тонюсеньких каблучках.

Все ей кажется ложью на свете,
все — от библии до газет.
Есть Монтекки и Капулетти.
Нет Ромео и нет Джульетт.

От раздумий деревья поникли,
и слоняется во хмелю
месяц, сумрачный, словно битник,
вдоль по млечному авеню.

Он бредет, как от стойки к стойке,
созерцающий нелюдим,
и прекрасный, но и жестокий
простирается город под ним.

Girl Beatnik

This girl comes from New York
but she does not belong.
Along the neon lights, this girl
runs away from herself.

To this girl the world seems odious—
a moralist who's been howled down.
It holds no more truths for her.
Now the "twist" alone is true.

With hair mussed and wild,
in spectacles and a coarse sweater,
on spiked heels she dances
the thinnest of negations.

Everything strikes her as false,
everything—from the Bible to the press.
The Montagues exist, and the Capulets,
but there are no Romeos and Juliets.

The trees stoop broodingly,
and rather drunkenly the moon
staggers like a beatnik sulking
along the milky avenue.

Wanders, as if from bar to bar,
wrapped in thought, unsocial,
and the city spreads underneath
in all its hard-hearted beauty.

Все жестоко — и крыши, и стены,
и над городом неспроста
телевизорные антенны
как распятия без Христа...

Нью-Йорк

All things look hard—the roofs and walls,
and it's no accident that, over the city,
the television antennae rise
like crucifixions without Christ.

New York 1961.

Монолог битников

«Двадцатый век нас часто одурачивал.
Нас, как налогом, ложью облагали.
Идеи с быстротою одуванчиков
от дуновенья жизни облетали.

И стала нам надежной обороною,
как едкая насмешливость — мальчишкам,
не слишком затаенная ирония,
но, впрочем, обнаженная не слишком.

Она была стеной или плотиною,
защиту от потока лжи даруя,
и руки усмехались, аплодируя,
и ноги ухмылялись, маршируя.

Могли писать о нас, экранизировать
написанную чушь — мы позволяли,
но право надо всем иронизировать
мы за собой тихонько оставляли.

Мы возвышались тем, что мы презрительны.
Все это так, но если углубиться,
ирония, из нашего спасителя
ты превратилась в нашего убийцу.

Мы любим лицемерно, настороженно.
Мы дружим половинчато, несмело,
и кажется нам наше настоящее
лишь прошлым, притворившимся умело.

Monologue of the Beatniks

The twentieth century has often fooled us.
We've been squeezed in by falsehood as by taxes.
The breath of life has denuded our ideas
as quickly as it strips a dandelion.

As boys fall back on biting sarcasm,
so we rely for our trusty armor
on an irony not too unobtrusive,
not too naked either.

It has served as a wall or dam
to shield us against a flood of lies,
and hands have laughed as they applauded,
and feet sniggered as they marched.

They could write about us, and we've allowed
them to make movies of this scribbled trash,
but we have reserved the right
to treat all this with quiet irony.

In our contempt we felt superior.
All this is so, but probing deeper,
irony, instead of acting as our saviour,
you have become our murderer.

We're cautious, hypocritical in love.
Our friendships are lukewarm, not brave,
and our present seems no different from
our past, so cunningly disguised.

Мы мечемся по жизни. Мы в истории,
как Фаусты, заранее подсудны.
Ирония с усмешкой Мефистофеля
как тень за нами следует повсюду.

Напрасно мы расстаться с нею пробуем.
Пути назад или вперед закрыты.
Ирония, тебе мы душу продали,
не получив за это Маргариты.

Мы заживо тобою похоронены.
Бессильны мы от горького познанья,
и наша же усталая ирония
сама иронизирует над нами».

Нью-Йорк

Through life we scurry. In history,
like any Faust, we've been pre-judged.
With Mephistophelian smile, irony,
like a shadow, dogs our every step.

In vain we try to dodge the shadow.
The paths in front, behind, are blocked.
Irony, to you we've sold our soul,
receiving no Margaret in return.

You have buried us alive.
Bitter knowledge has made us powerless,
and our weary irony
has turned against ourselves.

New York 1961.

Мед

Я расскажу вам быль про мед.
Пусть кой-кого она проймет,
пусть кто-то вроде не поймет,
что розговор о нем идет.
Итак,

      я расскажу про мед.
В том страшном,

               в сорок первом,

                        в Чистополе,
где голодало все и мерзло,
на снег базарный

                   бочку выставили
двадцативедерную! —

                 меда!
Был продавец из этой сволочи,
что наживается на горе,
и горе выстроилось в очередь,
простое,

        горькое,

              нагое.
Он не деньгами брал,

                 а кофтами,
часами

       или же отрезами.
Рука купеческая с кольцами
гнушалась явными отрепьями.
Он вещи на свету рассматривал.
Художник старый на ботинках
одной рукой шнурки разматывал,
другой —

         протягивал бутылку.

Honey

I shall tell you a true story about honey.
May it hit home in certain cases.
But someone may fail, as it were, to grasp
that we are talking of him.
Thus,
     let me tell you a tale of honey.
In that terrible year—
               in '41,
                      in Chistopol,
where everything was starved and frozen,
a barrel was put out
in the market snow—
twenty buckets full
           of honey!
The vendor was that sort of creep
who makes a profit out of grief,
and grief queued up in a long line,
plain,
     bitter,
          bare.
He took no cash,
           but bartered for blouses,
watches
     or cuts of cloth.
His trader's hand with many rings
spurned the obvious rags.
He raised each object to the light . . .
An aged artist with one hand
unlaced his boots,
and, in the other,
         held out a bottle.

Глядел, как мед тягуче цедится,
глядел согбенно и безропотно
и с медом —
                    с этой вечной ценностью —
по снегу шел в носках заштопанных.
Вокруг со взглядами стеклянными
солдат и офицеров жены
стояли с банками,
                    стаканами,
стояли немо,
                    напряженно.
И девочка
          прозрачной ручкой
в каком-то странном полусне
тянула крохотную рюмочку
с колечком маминым на дне.
Но —
          сани заскрипели мощно.
На спинке —
                    расписные розы.
И, важно лоб сановно морща,
сошел с них некто,
                    грузный,
                              рослый.
Большой,
          торжественный,
                              как в раме,
без тени жалости малейшей:
«Всю бочку.
          Заплачу коврами.
Давай сюда ее, милейший.

He watched the honey thickly dripping,
watched it, stooping, uncomplaining,
and then with the bottled honey—
                              that eternal value—
trudged through the snow in his darned socks.
All round with glazed eyes,
officers' and soldiers' wives
stood about with jars
                    and glasses,
stood dumb
          and tense.
And in her transparent hand a young girl,
a girl in a sort of strange and drowsy state,
held out a small wine glass
with her mother's little ring at the bottom.
But—
      a sleigh drew up with mighty creaking.
Roses were painted
                  on its back.
And wrinkling an imposing official brow,
A man descended,
                tall and heavy,
                                from the sleigh.
Large
      and solemn
                as a portrait in a frame,
without the least shade of pity he commanded:
"The whole barrel!
                  I'll settle with carpets.
Hoist it up here, my good fellow!"

Договоримся там,
                          на месте.
А ну-ка пособите, братцы...»
И укатили они вместе.
Они всегда договорятся.
Стояла очередь угрюмая,
ни в чем как будто не участвуя.
Колечко, выпавши из рюмочки,
упало в след саней умчавшихся...

Далек тот сорок первый год,
год отступлений и невзгод,
но жив он —
                          медолюбец тот,
и сладко до сих пор живет.
Когда степенно он несет
самоуверенный живот,
когда он смотрит на часы
и гладит сытые усы,
я вспоминаю этот год,
я вспоминаю этот мед.
Тот мед тогда
                          как будто сам
по этим,
                     этим тек усам.
С них никогда
                          он не сотрет
прилипший к ним
                               навеки
                                    мед!

We'll fix the price there,
                on the spot,
Well, give us a hand, brothers . . ."
And they drove off together.
They'll always be able to agree on a price.
Grimly the line of people stood
as if not involved.
The little ring, dropping from the wine glass,
fell in the wake of the scudding sleigh . . .

That year of '41 is now far off,
the year of misfortunes and retreats,
but he's still alive—
                that honey-sucker,
and lives sweetly in our day.
When staidly before him he carries
his bumptious belly,
when he glances at his watch
and strokes his satiate mustaches,
I recall that year,
remember that honey.
That honey seemed
                to flow freely then
over those,
            over those mustaches flowing.
From them
        he will never wipe away
the honey
        stuck to them
                    forever!

1961 [1962].

Ограда

В. Луговскому

Могила,
      ты ограблена оградой.
Ограда, отделила ты его
от грома грузовых,
             от груш,
                    от града
агатовых смородин.
          От всего,
что в нем переливалось, мчалось, билось,
как искры из-под бешеных копыт.
Все это было буйный быт —
                 не бытность.
И битвы —
          это тоже было быт.
Был хряск рессор
                и взрывы конских храпов,
покой прудов
                и сталкиванье льдов,
азарт базаров
                и сохранность храмов,
прибой садов
              и груды городов.
Подарок — делать созданный подарки,
камнями и корнями покорен,
он, словно странник, проходил по давке
из-за кормов и крошечных корон.
Он шел,
      другим оставив суетиться.
Крепка была походка и легка
серебряноголового артиста
со смуглыми щеками моряка.

The Railing

TO V. LUGOVSKOY

Grave,
            reived by a railing.
Railing, you've cut him off
from the growling trucks,
                        good pears,
                                    the gashing hail
of agate currants.
                    From everything
in him that brimmed over, pounded, spurted,
like sparks beneath the brawling hooves.
All this was boisterous being—
                            no bland existence.
And battles, too,
                were common life.
There were creaking carriage springs
                and bursts of horses' snorting,
the peace of ponds,
                    the crump of crashing icefloes,
the hazard of bazaars,
                        the integrity of temples,
gardens in full blow,
                    and clumps of cities.
A gift—created to bestow more gifts,
now routed by stone and root,
he, like a pilgrim, had stepped over the crush
for provender and petty crowns.
He went his way,
                leaving all the fuss to others.
Firm and springy was the stride
of this silver-headed author
with a sailor's swarthy cheeks.

Пушкинианец, вольно и велико
он и у тяжких горестей в кольце
был как большая детская улыбка
у мученика века на лице.
И знаю я — та тихая могила
не пристань для печальных чьих-то лиц.
Она навек неистово магнитна
для мальчиков, цветов, семян и птиц.
Могила,

            ты ограблена оградой,
но видел я в осенней тишине:
там две сосны растут, как сестры, рядом —
одна в ограде и другая вне.
И непреоборимыми рывками,
ограду обвиняя в воровстве,
та, что в ограде, тянется руками
к не огражденной от людей сестре.
Не помешать ей никакою рубкой!
Обрубят ветви —

                    отрастут опять.
И кажется мне —

                    это его руки
людей и сосны тянутся обнять.
Всех тех, кто жил, как он, другим наградой,
от горестей земных, земных отрад
не отгородишь никакой оградой.
На свете нет еще таких оград.

Lover of Pushkin, willingly and greatly,
even though penned in by grievous griefs,
he was a large, childlike smile
upon the face of the martyr age.
And this I know--that tranquil grave
affords no haven for some mourning faces.
For ages it will be an irrational magnet
for boys, flowers, seeds and birds . . .
Grave,
          reived by a railing,
in the autumn silence I have seen
two pines, like sisters, growing side by side—
one pine within, the other outside the railing.
And with irrepressible thrusts
accusing the railing as a reiver,
the imprisoned pine holds out her arms
to her unimprisoned sister.
No pruning can hinder that!
Hew them off—
                    and branches will grow again.
Those are his arms—
                    it seems—
reaching out to embrace both pines and people.
No railing, you find, will isolate
any man who has lived, as he, gift to his fellows,
from this earth's griefs, this earth's consolations.
As yet this world has no such railings.

1961

Град в Харькове

В граде Харькове —
                               град.
Крупен град,
                   как виноград.
Он танцует у оград,
пританцо-вы-ва-ет.
Он шустер и шаловат,
и сам черт ему не брат.
В губы градины летят
леденцовые!
Града стукот,
                     града цокот
по зальделой мостовой.
Деревянный круглый цоколь
покидает постовой.
Постовой,
               постовой,
а дорожит головой!

Вот блатной мордастый жлоб
жмется к магазинчику.
Град ему как вдарит в лоб —
сбил малокозырочку!

Вот шагает в гости попик.
Поиграть идет он в покер.
Град как попику поддаст!
И совсем беспомощно
попик прячется в подъезд
«Общества безбожников».

Hail in Kharkov

In the burgh of Kharkov—
                                    bursting hail.
Big hail,
            big as grape,
and it goes dancing along the railings,
dancing, prancing.
It's spry and full of pranks,
and the devil's no match for it.
Like fruit-candy, lumps of hail
assail the lips.
Hail spatters,
                    clatters,
on the glazing pavement.
The traffic cop jumps off
his round wooden stand.
Cop, cop,
            traffic cop,
but he wants to guard his head.

There goes a hoodlum with heavy jowl
squirming up to a little shop.
The hail—it biffs him on the brow,
knocking off his small peaked cap!

There goes a priest out visiting.
He's off to play a game of poker.
The hail gives the priest what-ho!
And quite helplessly the priest
takes shelter in the entrance to
"The Society of the Godless".

Вот бежит филологичка.
Град шибает здорово!
Совершенно алогично
вдруг косынку сдергивает.
Пляшут чертики в глазах,
пляшут, как на празднике,
и сверкают в волосах
светляками градинки...

Человек в универмаге
приобрел китайский таз.
На тазу у него маки...
Вдруг по тазу град как даст!
Таз поет,
                звенит,
                        грохочет...
Человек идет,
                хохочет.
Град игрив,
                задирист,
                        буен...
Еще раз!
        Еще раз!
Таз играет, словно бубен,
хоть иди пляши под таз!
Град идет!
        Град!
                Град!
Град, давай,
        тебе я рад!

There, running, goes a girl philologist.
The hail gives her a hefty whacking!
Of a sudden, quite alogically,
it jerks her plaits awry.
In one's eyes skip little devils,
dancing as at a festival,
and globules of hail,
like glow-worms, glisten in one's hair.

In the Univermag a man
has just acquired a Chinese basin
with poppies painted on it.
Suddenly the hail starts banging on the basin!
The basin sings,
            dings,
                   dongs . . .
The man walks on,
                guffawing.
Hail's a prankster,
               cheeky,
                   wild . . .
Once again!
         Once again!
The basin sounds a tambourine,
go and dance to it, you can.
Hail pelts down!
           Hail!
             Hail!
Let me tell you, hail,
           I'm glad!

Все, кто молод,

             граду рады,

пусть сильней хоть во сто крат!

Через разные преграды

я иду вперед

                сквозь град,

град насмешек,

              сплетен хитрых,

что летят со всех сторон.

Град опасен лишь для хилых.

А для сильных нужен он!

Град не грусть,

              а град награда

не боящимся преград.

Улыбаться надо граду,

чтобы радостью был град!

Град, давай!

All who are young,
                        are glad of hail,
even when a hundred times more strong!
Over all sorts of barriers
I stride ahead
                        through hail,
the hail of gibes,
                        of crafty slanders,
which assail me on every side.
Hail is dangerous only for the weak.
But the strong have need of it.
Hail is nothing sad,
                        hail is a reward
to those who fear no barriers.
One should greet hail smiling,
hail should give great joy!
Hail, do your best!

1961.

Бабий яр

Над Бабьим Яром памятников нет.
Крутой обрыв, как грубое надгробье.
Мне страшно.

                Мне сегодня столько лет,
как самому еврейскому народу.
Мне кажется сейчас —

                    я иудей.
Вот я бреду по древнему Египту.
А вот я, на кресте распятый, гибну,
и до сих пор на мне — следы гвоздей.
Мне кажется, что Дрейфус —

                      это я.
Мещанство —

           мой доносчик и судья.
Я за решеткой.

             Я попал в кольцо.
Затравленный,

            оплеванный,

                  оболганный.
И дамочки с брюссельскими оборками,
визжа, зонтами тычут мне в лицо.
Мне кажется —

             я мальчик в Белостоке.
Кровь льется, растекаясь по полам.
Бесчинствуют вожди трактирной стойки
и пахнут водкой с луком пополам.
Я, сапогом отброшенный, бессилен.
Напрасно я погромщиков молю.
Под гогот:

         «Бей жидов, спасай Россию!»
Лабазник избивает мать мою.

Babii Yar

No monument stands over Babii Yar.
A drop sheer as a crude gravestone.
I am afraid.
         Today I am as old in years
as all the Jewish people.
Now I seem to be
         a Jew.
Here I plod through ancient Egypt.
Here I perish crucified, on the cross,
and to this day I bear the scars of nails.
I seem to be
         Dreyfus.
The Philistine
         is both informer and judge.
I am behind bars.
         Beset on every side.
Hounded,
      spat on,
         slandered.
Squealing, dainty ladies in flounced Brussels lace
stick their parasols into my face.
I seem to be then
         a young boy in Byelostok.
Blood runs, spilling over the floors.
The bar-room rabble-rousers
give off a stench of vodka and onion.
A boot kicks me aside, helpless.
In vain I plead with these pogrom bullies.
While they jeer and shout,
         "Beat the Yids. Save Russia!"
some grain-marketeer beats up my mother.

О, русский мой народ!

    Я знаю —

          ты

по сущности интернационален.

Но часто те, чьи руки не чисты,

твоим чистейшим именем бряцали.

Я знаю доброту моей земли.

Как подло,

    что, и жилочкой не дрогнув,

антисемиты пышно нарекли

себя «Союзом русского народа»!

Мне кажется —

      я — это Анна Франк,

прозрачная,

      как веточка в апреле.

И я люблю.

    И мне не надо фраз.

Мне надо,

    чтоб друг в друга мы смотрели.

Как мало можно видеть,

        обонять!

Нельзя нам листьев

      и нельзя нам неба.

Но можно очень много —

        это нежно

друг друга в темной комнате обнять.

Сюда идут?

    Не бойся — это гулы

самой весны —

      она сюда идет.

Иди ко мне.

O my Russian people!
                    I know
                              you
are international to the core.
But those with unclean hands
have often made a jingle of your purest name.
I know the goodness of my land.
How vile these antisemites—
                              without a qualm
they pompously called themselves
"The Union of the Russian People"!
I seem to be
          Anne Frank
transparent
              as a branch in April.
And I love.
          And have no need of phrases.
My need
          is that we gaze into each other.
How little we can see
                    or smell!
We are denied the leaves,
                    we are denied the sky.
Yet we can do so much—
                    tenderly
embrace each other in a dark room.
They're coming here?
                    Be not afraid. Those are the booming
sounds of spring:
                    spring is coming here.
Come then to me.

Дай мне скорее губы.
Ломают дверь?

            Нет — это ледоход...
Над Бабьим Яром шелест диких трав.
Деревья смотрят грозно,

                   по-судейски.
Все молча здесь кричит,

                и, шапку сняв,
я чувствую,

          как медленно седею.
И сам я,

        как сплошной беззвучный крик,
над тысячами тысяч погребенных.
Я —
каждый здесь расстрелянный

                   старик.
Я —
каждый здесь расстрелянный

                  ребенок.
Ничто во мне

          про это не забудет!
«Интернационал»

            пусть прогремит,
когда навеки похоронен будет
последний на земле антисемит.
Еврейской крови нет в крови моей.
Но ненавистен злобой заскорузлой
я всем антисемитам, как еврей.
И потому —

          я настоящий русский!

Quick, give me your lips.
Are they smashing down the door?
                              No, it's the ice breaking . . .
The wild grasses rustle over Babii Yar.
The trees look ominous,
                    like judges.
Here all things scream silently,
                         and, baring my head,
slowly I feel myself
                turning gray.
And I myself
             am one massive, soundless scream
above the thousand thousand buried here.
I am
      each old man
                     here shot dead.
I am
      every child
                    here shot dead.
Nothing in me
              shall ever forget!
The "Internationale", let it
                            thunder
when the last antisemite on earth
is buried forever.
In my blood there is no Jewish blood.
In their callous rage, all antisemites
must hate me now as a Jew.
For that reason
               I am a true Russian!

September 19, 1961.

Разговор с американским писателем

«Мне говорят —
                    ты смелый человек.
Неправда.

                    Никогда я не был смелым.
Считал я просто недостойным делом
унизиться до трусости коллег.

Устоев никаких не потрясал.
Смеялся просто над фальшивым,

                                        дутым.
Писал статьи.

                    Доносов не писал.
И говорить старался

                        все, что думал.
Да,

    защищал талантливых людей,
клеймил бездарных,

                        лезущих в писатели,
но делать это, в общем, обязательно,
а мне твердят о смелости моей.
О, вспомнят с чувством горького стыда
потомки наши,

                    расправляясь с мерзостью,
то время,

            очень странное,

                                когда
простую честность

                    называли смелостью...»

Нью-Йорк

Conversation with an American Writer

"You have courage,"
                    they tell me.

It's not true.
                    I was never courageous.
I simply felt it unbecoming
to stoop to the cowardice of my colleagues.

I've shaken no foundations.
I simply mocked at pretense
                                    and inflation.
Wrote articles.
                    Scribbled no denunciations.
And tried to speak all
                    on my mind.
Yes,
      I defended men of talent,
branding the hacks,
                    the would-be writers.
But this, in general, we should always do;
and yet they keep stressing my courage.
Oh, our descendants will burn with bitter shame
to remember, when punishing vile acts,
that most peculiar
                    time,
                            when
plain honesty
            was labeled "courage"...

New York 1961.

Поэзия —

        не мирная молельня.

Поэзия —

        жестокая война.

В ней есть свои, обманные маневры.

Война —

      она войною быть должна.

Поэт —

     солдат,

          и все он делать вправе,

когда он прав,

        идя в огонь и дым.

Поступки тех,

       кто на переднем крае,

понять ли жалким крысам тыловым?

От фронта в отдалении позорном

они крысиным скепсисом больны.

Им,

   крысам,

       смелость кажется позерством

и трусостью —

         стратегия борьбы.

Кричать герою: «Трус!» —

          попытка трусов

себя возвысить,

       над героем встать.

Поэт

    как ясновидящий Кутузов.

Он отступает,

       чтобы наступать.

Он изнемог.

Poetry

Poetry
  is no chapel of peace.
Poetry
  is savage war.
It has its own manoeuvres of deception.
War
    must be war.
A poet
    is a soldier
                  and, when he's right,
he's right to try all things
                  when going through smoke and fire.
How should the slinking rats in the rear
understand how men
                  act under fire?
At a safe distance from the front,
they're sick with a ratlike skepsis.
To them,
      the rats,
                courage seems a pose,
and the strategy of struggle
                  mere cowardice.
To brand a hero "Coward!"
                    is the coward's attempt
to raise himself,
          to top the hero.
The poet
      is like Kutuzov the clearsighted.
He retreats
      in order to advance.
Exhausted,

Он выпьет полколодца.

Он хочет спать.

Но суть его сама

ему велит глазами полководца

глядеть на время с некого холма.

В движение орудья,

             фуры,

                   флаги

приводит его властная рука.

Пускай считают, что на правом фланге

сосредоточил он свои войска.

Но он-то,

        он-то знает,

                 что на левом,

с рассвета ожидая трубача,

готова к бою

          конница за лесом,

ноздрями упоенно трепеща.

Поэт воюет

не во имя славы

и всяческих чинов и орденов.

Лгут на него.

        И слева лгут,

                и справа,

но он с презреньем смотрит на лгунов.

Ну а когда поэт —

         он погибает,

и мертвый

        он внушает им испуг.

Он погибает так, как подобает, —

оружия не выпустив из рук.

he drains half a well.
He wants to sleep.
But with a commander-in-chief's eyes
his essential self commands him to look
at time from a certain eminence.
His powerful hand
sets in motion the guns,
                        the baggage-trains,
                                        the flags.
Let them think he has concentrated
his troops on the right flank.
But as for him,
                he knows
                        that, to the left,
awaiting the bugle call since dawn,
the cavalry strains behind the wood
                                with quivering nostrils,
ready for the charge.
The poet fights
                not in glory's name,
nor for rank or orders.
They slander him.
                They slander him from left,
                                        and right,
but he looks down on the liars with contempt.
Well, when a poet. . .
                        a poet perishes,
even in death
                he inspires them with fear.
He perishes as behooves him—
without dropping his weapons.

Его глаза боится тронуть ворон.
Поэт глядит,

         всевидяще суров,
и даже мертвый —

              он все тот же воин,
и даже мертвый —

             страшен для врагов.

The raven fears to peck at his eyes.
All seeing and austere,
                        the poet gazes,
and even in death
                he is ever the same warrior,
and even in death
                his enemies' terror.

1962.

Стук в дверь

«Кто там?» —

«Я старость.

Я к тебе пришла».

«Потом.

Я занят.

У меня дела».

Писал.

Звонил.

Уничтожал омлет.

Открыл я дверь,

но никого там нет.

Шутили, может, надо мной друзья?

А может, имя не расслышал я?!

Не старость —

это зрелость здесь была,

не дождалась,

вздохнула

и ушла?!

A Knock on the Door

"Who's there?"
                    "I'm old age,
                              I've come to see you."
"Later!
        I'm busy.
                    I've things to do!"
I wrote.
        Telephoned.
                    Demolished a fried egg.
Then I opened the door,
                    but found no one there.
Maybe friends were pulling my leg?
Or perhaps I hadn't heard the name right.
It wasn't old age,
                but maturity, had called.
It couldn't wait,
            sighed,
                    and departed.

1961 [1962].

Наследники Сталина

Безмолствовал мрамор.

          Безмолвно мерцало стекло.

Безмолвно стоял караул,

          на ветру бронзовея.

А гроб чуть дымился.

          Дыханье сквозь щели текло,

когда выносили его из дверей Мавзолея.

Гроб медленно плыл,

          задевая краями штыки.

Он тоже безмолвным был —

          тоже!

          но грозно безмолвным.

Угрюмо сжимая

          набальзамированные кулаки,

в нем к щели приник

          человек, притворившийся мертвым.

Хотел он запомнить всех тех,

          кто его выносил:

рязанских и курских молоденьких

          новобранцев,

чтоб как-нибудь после

          набраться для вылазки сил,

и встать из земли,

          и до них неразумных добраться.

Он что-то задумал.

          Он лишь отдохнуть прикорнул.

И я обращаюсь к правительству нашему

          с просьбою:

удвоить,

     утроить

          у этой плиты караул,

чтоб Сталин не встал,

The Heirs of Stalin

Mute was the marble.
                    Mutely glimmered the glass.
Mute stood the sentries,
                    bronzed by the breeze.
Thin wisps of smoke curled over the coffin.
                    And breath seeped through the chinks
as they bore him out the mausoleum doors.
Slowly the coffin floated,
                    grazing the fixed bayonets.
He also was mute—
            he also!—
                    mute and dread.
Grimly clenching
            his embalmed fists,
just pretending to be dead,
                    he watched from inside.
He wished to fix each pallbearer
                    in his memory:
young recruits
            from Ryazan and Kursk,
so that later he might
                    collect enough strength for a sortie,
rise from the grave,
                    and reach these unreflecting youths.
He was scheming.
            Had merely dozed off.
And I, appealing to our government,
                    petition them
to double,
            and treble,
                    the sentries guarding this slab,
and stop Stalin from ever rising again

и со Сталиным —

                    прошлое.

Я речь не о том сокровенном и доблестном

                              прошлом веду,

где были Турксиб,

и Магнитка,

и флаг над Берлином.

Я в случае данном

                    под прошлым имею в виду

забвенье о благе народа,

                       наветы,

                              аресты безвинных.

Мы сеяли честно.

Мы честно варили металл

и честно шагали мы,

                    строясь в солдатские цепи.

А он нас боялся.

                  Он, веря в великую цель, не считал,

что средства

                должны быть достойны

величия цели.

Он был дальновиден.

               В законах борьбы умудрен,

наследников многих на шаре земном он

                        оставил.

Мне чудится,

           будто поставлен в гробу телефон:

Энверу Ходжа

              сообщает свои указания Сталин.

Куда еще тянется провод из гроба того!

Нет, — Сталин не сдался.

and, with Stalin,

the past.

I refer not to the past,

so holy and glorious,

of Turksib,

and Magnitka,

and the flag raised over Berlin.

By the past, in this case,

I mean the neglect

of the people's good,

false charges,

the jailing of innocent men.

We sowed our crops honestly.

Honestly we smelted metal,

and honestly we marched,

joining the ranks.

But he feared us.

Believing in the great goal,

he judged

all means justified

to that great end.

He was far-sighted.

Adept in the art of political warfare,

he left many heirs

behind on this globe.

I fancy

there's a telephone in that coffin:

Stalin instructs

Enver Hoxha.

From that coffin where else does the cable go!

No, Stalin has not given up.

Считает он смерть —

                        поправимостью.
Мы вынесли

                из Мавзолея

                                его.
Но как из наследников Сталина

                        Сталина вынести?!
Иные наследники розы в отставке стригут,
а втайне считают,

                что временна эта отставка.
Иные

        и Сталина даже ругают с трибун,
а сами

        ночами

                тоскуют о времени старом.
Наследников Сталина, видно, сегодня не зря
хватают инфаркты.

                        Им бывшим когда-то опорами,
не нравится время,

                в котором пусты лагеря,
а залы, где слушают люди стихи, —

                        переполнены.
Велела

        не быть успокоенным

                        Партия мне.
Пусть кто-то твердит:

                «Успокойся!» — спокойным я быть

                                не сумею.
Покуда наследники Сталина есть на земле,
мне будет казаться,

                что Сталин еще в Мавзолее.

                      He thinks he can
                                        cheat death.
We carried
          him
                   from the mausoleum.
But how remove Stalin's heirs
                         from Stalin!
Some of his heirs tend roses in retirement,
thinking in secret
                        their enforced leisure will not last.
Others,
          from platforms, even heap abuse on Stalin
but,
      at night,
                    yearn for the good old days.
No wonder Stalin's heirs seem to suffer
these days from heart trouble.
                            They, the former henchmen,
hate this era
               of emptied prison camps
and auditoriums full of people listening
                              to poets.
The Party
          discourages me
                       from being smug.
"Why care?"
               some say, but I can't remain
                                        inactive.
While Stalin's heirs walk this earth,
Stalin,
       I fancy, still lurks in the mausoleum.
1962.

Я — Ангел

Не пью.

      Люблю свою жену.

Свою —

      я это акцентирую.

Я так по-ангельски живу —

чуть Щипачева не цитирую.

От этой жизни я зачах.

На женщин всех глаза закрыл я.

Неловкость чувствую в плечах.

Ого!

      Растут, наверно, крылья!

Я растерялся.

        Я в тоске.

Растут — зануды!

        Дело скверно!

Теперь придется в пиджаке

проделать прорези, наверно.

Я ангел.

      Жизни не корю

за все жестокие обидности.

Я ангел.

      Только вот курю.

Я —

      из курящей разновидности.

Быть ангелом —

        страннейший труд.

Лишь дух один.

        Ни грамма тела.

И мимо женщины идут.

Я ангел.

      Что со мной им делать!

I'm an Angel

I've stopped drinking.
                    I love my wife.
My own wife—
                    I insist on this.
Living so like an angel,
I almost quote Shchipachev.
This is a shriveled life.
I've shut my eyes to all other women.
My shoulders feel peculiar.
Aha!
       Wings must be sprouting!
This makes me anxious.
                         Moody.
And the wings keep sprouting—what a nuisance!
                                    How awkward!
Now I'll have to slit
my jacket in appropriate places.
A true angel,
             I bear life no grudge
for all its cruel hurts.
I'm a true angel.
                   But I still smoke.
I'm the smoking type.
To be an angel
                is strange work.
Pure spirit.
             Not an ounce of flesh.
And the women pass by.
A true angel,
             what good to them am I!

Пока что я для них не в счет,
пока что я в небесном ранге,
но самый страшный в жизни черт,
учтите, —
                это бывший ангел!

I don't count for the present,
not while I hold celestial rank,
but—bear in mind—in this life,
a fallen angel
                is the worst devil of all!

1962.

IV. People Were Laughing:
Poems 1963–1965

"I have returned in no good standing,
And after some sharp reprimands . . ."

Опять на станции Зима

Боюсь, читатель, ты ладонью
прикроешь тягостность зевка.
Прости мне кровь мою чалдонью,
но я тебе опять далдоню
про ту же станцию Зима.

Зима! Вокзальчик с палисадом,
деревьев чахлых с полдесятка,
в мешках колхозниц поросята...
И замедляет поезд ход,
и пассажиры волосато,
в своих пижамах полосатых,
как тигры, прыгают вперед.

Вот по перрону резво рыщет,
роняя тапочки, толстяк.
Он жилковатым носом свищет.
Он весь в поту. Он пива ищет
и не найдет его никак.

И после долгого опроса,
пыхтя, как после опороса,
вокзальчик взглядом смерит косо:
«Ну и дырища! Ну и грязь!»
В перрон вминает папиросу,
бредет в купе и, под колеса,
как в транс, впадает в преферанс.

Again at Zima Station *

I'm afraid, dear reader, with your hand
you'll stifle a rising yawn.
Forgive me my Siberian blood,
but here I'm harping to you again
about the Zima Station you know of old.

Zima! a station small with palisade,
half-a-dozen drooping trees,
and a Kholhoz woman with porkers in a sack . . .
And then the train starts slowing down,
and wild-haired passengers
in brightly striped pajamas leap
ahead like so many tigers.

There, on the railroad platform, a fat
man petulantly prowls, losing his sneakers.
He wheezes through his sinewy nose.
He's all in sweat. He's seeking beer,
and he can't find it for all his effort.

Then, after many inquiries,
and puffing as though he'd farrowed,
he glances round the station with disgust:
"Well, what a hole! A filthy hole!"
Crushing a butt against the platform,
he finds his seat and, to the chug of wheels,
as in a trance sinks down to *preference.*

---
* *Here are two distinct passages from a longer poem. See the Introduction
and the Notes.*

А ведь родился-то, наверно,
и не в Париже и не в Вене,
а, скажем, где-нибудь в Клинцах.
И пусть уж он тогда не взыщет,
что и в Клинцах такой же рыщет
и на перроне пива ищет,
и не найдя, — «ну и дырища!» —
его Клинцы клянет в сердцах...

О, это мелочное чванство,
в нем столько жалкого мещанства!
Оно позор перед страной,
страной огромной, неустанной,
где каждый малый полустанок —
он для кого-нибудь родной.

И, даже мчась куда-то мимо,
должны мы в помыслах своих
родным, от нас неотделимым
считать родное для других.

. . . .

И как бы мог любить я Кубу,
ее оливковую куртку,
ее деревья и дома,
когда бы нежно и кристально
я, как Есенин мать-крестьянку,
не обожал тебя, Зима?

Мое любое возвращенье
к тебе всегда, как возрожденье,

But probably he was not born
in Paris, or even in Vienna,
but, let us say, somewhere in Klintzi.
He therefore should not object
if a man like him now prowls in Klintzi,
searching for beer along the platform,
and, failing to find it, mutters: "What a hole!"
and curses this Klintzi in his heart.

Oh, this conceit, so small, so trifling—
it reeks of much that's petty bourgeois!
In our country's face it's sheer disgrace—
a country vast and inexhaustible,
where each small local station means
so much to anyone who holds it dear.

When we rush by in some direction,
we should, pursuing our designs,
regard what's dear to others as
dear to and inseparable from us.

.   .   .   .

However much I may love Cuba,
her jacket of olive color,
her houses and her trees,
yet with a crystal love, and tender,
when have I not adored you, Zima station,
as Yesenin did his peasant mother?!

Whenever I come back to you, Zima,
I always feel as though reborn,

и с новым смыслом каждый раз.
И вот в Зиме я вновь сейчас.

Я возвратился после странствий,
покрытый пылью Англий, Франций
да пылью слухов обо мне
и — буду прям — не на коне.

Я возвратился не в почете,
а после критики крутой,
полезной нам в конечном счете...
И с лаской принят был роднёй

И дядя мой Андрей в итоге
сказал такие мне слова:
«Не раскисай! Есть руки, ноги
и даже вроде голова.

Какой ты должен сделать вывод?
Работа — вот, племянник, выход.
Закон у нас хороший есть:
«Кто не работает — не ест!»

and gain a sense of something new.
So here I am in Zima once again.

After many journeys I've returned,
covered with the dust of England, France,
and with the dust of rumors about myself,
and—frankly—not in triumph on a charger.

I have returned in no good standing,
and after some sharp reprimands,
which have their use in the final count . . .
But relatives received me with affection.

My uncle Andrey then toted up
the balance, and declared as follows:
"Do not turn sour! You still have hands
and feet, and even a head of sorts.

"And what conclusion must you draw?
Work is the best way out, my nephew.
We have a law, good law, that says:
'He shall not eat, who does no work!' "

August, 1963.

Нет, мне ни в чем не надо половины!

Нет, мне ни в чем не надо половины!
Мне — дай все небо! Землю всю положь!
Моря и реки, горные лавины —
мои! Не соглашаюсь на дележ!

Нет, жизнь, меня ты не заластишь частью.
Все полностью! Мне это по плечу.
Я не хочу ни половины счастья,
ни половины горя не хочу!

Хочу лишь половину той подушки,
где, бережно прижатое к щеке,
беспомощной звездой, звездой падучей
кольцо мерцает на твоей руке...

No, I'll Not Take the Half

No, I'll not take the half of anything!
Give me the whole sky! The far flung earth!
Seas and rivers and mountain avalanches—
All these are mine! I'll accept no less!

No, life, you cannot woo me with a part.
Let it be all or nothing! I can shoulder that!
I don't want happiness by halves,
Nor is half of sorrow what I want.

Yet there's a pillow I would share,
Where gently pressed against a cheek,
Like a helpless star, a falling star,
A ring glimmers on a finger of your hand.

1963.

Смеялись люди за стеной

Смеялись люди за стеной,
а я глядел на эту стену
с душой, как с девочкой больной
в руках, пустевших постепенно.

Смеялись люди за стеной.
Они как будто измывались.
Они смеялись надо мной,
и как бессовестно смеялись!

На самом деле там, в гостях,
устав кружиться по паркету,
они смеялись просто так,
не надо мной и не над кем-то.

Да, так устроен шар земной
и так устроен будет вечно:
рыдает кто-то за стеной,
когда смеемся мы беспечно.

Но так устроен шар земной
и тем вовек неувядаем:
смеется кто-то за стеной,
когда мы чуть ли не рыдаем.

Двойной исполнись доброты.
И, чтоб кого-то не обидеть,
когда смеешься громко ты,
умей сквозь стену сердцем видеть.

People Were Laughing Behind a Wall

People were laughing behind a wall,
and I stared hard at that very wall,
while my soul was like an ailing girl
in arms that gradually felt emptier.

People were laughing behind a wall.
They seemed to be making fun of me.
I was the butt of all their laughter,
and how dishonestly they laughed!

But, in reality, they were but guests,
who, tired of shuffling round the floor,
were laughing to while the time away,
and not personally at me or anybody else.

People were laughing behind a wall,
warming themselves with wine,
and, laughing, they did not suspect at all
my presence there with my ailing soul.

People were laughing . . . How many times
have I also laughed like that myself,
while someone lay dying behind a wall,
painfully reconciling himself to this.

And he was thinking, by misfortune tracked,
and almost on the point of giving in,
that it was I who laughed at him,
and even mocked him, it would seem.

Смеялись люди за стеной,
себя вином подогревали
и обо мне с моей больной,
смеясь, и не подозревали.

Смеялись люди... Сколько раз
я тоже, тоже так смеялся,
а за стеною кто-то гас
и с этим горестно смирялся.

И думал он, бедой гоним
и ей почти уже сдаваясь,
что это я смеюсь над ним
и, может, даже издеваюсь.

Но не прими на душу грех,
когда ты мрачный и разбитый,
там, за стеною, чей-то смех
сочесть завистливо обидой.

Как равновесье — бытие.
В нем зависть — самооскорбленье.
Ведь за несчастие твое
чужое счастье — искупленье.

Желай, чтоб в час последний твой,
когда замрут глаза, смыкаясь, —
смеялись люди за стеной,
смеялись, все-таки смеялись!

Yes, this is how our globe's arranged,
and will be thus arranged forever:
sobs will sound behind a wall
when nonchalantly we begin to laugh.

But also the globe is so arranged,
and thus will never evanesce:
someone will always laugh behind a wall
when we're about to break out sobbing.

Double your kindness, be fulfilled,
and to avoid offending any person,
allow your heart to see right through a wall
when noisily you burst out laughing.

But, feeling broken and depressed,
do not impose, from envy, on your soul
the sin of regarding it as an offense
when someone laughs behind a wall.

Existence is an equilibrium of sorts.
A show of envy is an insult to oneself.
Another's happiness will expiate
for any misfortune you might suffer.

In your last hour when closing eyes
grow glazed, express your final wish:
let people laugh behind a wall,
let them laugh indeed, laugh if they must!

1963.

Ах, как ты, речь моя, слаба!

Ах, как ты, речь моя, слаба!
Ах, как никчемны, непричемны,
как непросторны все слова
перед просторами Печоры!

Но веры требуя в себя,
вовсю дымя непобедимо,
на Юг торопятся суда,
собой расталкивая льдины.

И над прыжками оленят,
последним снегом окропленные,
на Север лебеди летят,
как будто льдины окрыленные.

Печора плещется, дразня:
«Ну что ты плачешься сопливо?
Боишься, что ли, ты меня?
Шагни ко мне, шагни с обрыва...»

И я в Печору прыгнул так,
забыв легко про все былое,
как сиганул Иван-дурак
в котел с кипящею смолою,

чтоб выйти гордым силачом,
в кафтане новеньком, посмеиваясь,
и чуть поигрывать плечом:
«А ну-ка, силами померяйтесь!»

Ah, How Faltering You Are, My Speech

Ah, how faltering you are, my speech!
Ah, how good-for-nothing, insignificant,
how unexpansive are all words when faced
with the wide expanses of the Pechora!

But exacting our devout faith,
unconquerably belching smoke,
steamers go hurrying to the South,
heaving great blocks of ice aside.

And above the hoof-marks of leaping does,
now strewn over by the last fall of snow,
the swans, resembling blocks of ice
with wings, are flying to the North.

With its splashing waters, the Pechora teases:
"Well, why do you snivel? Why do you weep?
Are you afraid, afraid of me, perhaps?
Step then, step toward me from the steep . . ."

And I took such a header into the Pechora,
easily forgetting all that went before,
I might well have been Ivan-the-Fool
nipping into a cauldron of boiling pitch,

to emerge therefrom a cocksure, brawny man,
smiling confidently in a new caftan,
and twitching a shoulder as if to say:
"Well, would you like to try your strength!"

1964.

Зрелость любви?

Это что ж?

           Значит, зрелость любви?

Вот я сжался,

        я жду.

             Ты идешь.

Встреча взглядов!

            Должен быть вздрог!

Но — покой...

          как удар под вздох!

Встреча пальцев!

            Должен быть взрыв!!!

Но — покой...

          Я бегу, чуть не взвыв.

Значит, все —

         для тебя и меня?

Значит, пепел —

          зрелость огня?

Значит, зрелость любви —

                просто родственность,

да и то —

          еще в лучшем случае?

Это кто же над нами юродствует,

усмехаясь усмешкой злючею?

Кто же выдумать мог посметь

лживый термин в холодной умелости?

У любви есть рожденье и смерть.

У люби не бывает зрелости.

И грохочет любовь,

               расшуровывая

нам грозящее затухание,

и она —

Love's Maturity

Love's maturity, you say?
                            Is that so?
Straining,
        I wait.
             You come.
Glances meet!
          No shudder even!
Instead, repose . . .
              as though winded by a blow.
Fingers touch!
          No explosion even! ! !
Instead, repose . . .
             ready to howl, I run.
Is that all
        between you and me?
Are ashes
        the maturity of fire then?
Is love's maturity
            nò more than affinity,
and that only
           in the best of cases?
Who's playing the monster over us,
wicked and leering?
Who, with cold efficacy,
dared fabricate a false definition?
Love has its birth and death.
Love has no maturity.
Love roars,
        stoking
the menace of extinction for us,
and it breathes

не дыхание ровное,
а хрипящее задыхание,
как хрипит —
                и пощады моля,
и нещады, —
                рассудком оставленная,
задыхающаяся земля,
мирозданьем полураздавленная...

        not with equanimity,
but huskily
gasps—
      begging for mercy
and no mercy—
         as the stifling earth gasps,
abandoned by reason,
half-smothered by the world's creation . . .

1964.

Нефертити

Как ни крутите,
                        ни вертите, —
существовала Нефертити.

Она когда-то в мире оном
жила с каким-то фараоном,
но даже если с ним лежала,
она векам принадлежала.

И он испытывал страданья
от видимости обладанья.

Носил он важно облаченья.
Произносил он обличенья,
он укреплял свои устои,
но, как заметил Авиценна,
в природе рядом с красотою
любая власть неполноценна.
И фараона мучил комплекс
неполноценности... Он комкал
ковер ногою за обедом,
когда раздумывал об этом.

Имел он войско,
                        колесницы,
ну, а она —
                        глаза, ресницы,
и лоб,
            звездами озаренный,
и шеи выгиб изумленный.

Nefertiti

Turn as you may,
                    and twist,
Nefertiti did exist.

In this world upon a time
with a pharaoh she lived;
but though she shared his couch,
the future ages to her laid claim.

His so manifest possessions
were a source of worry to him.

With dignity he wore his vestments,
and pronounced his condemnations;
he kept strengthening his foundations,
but, as Avicenna once remarked,
when, in nature, authority comes face to face
with beauty, its value depreciates.
And the pharaoh was much tormented
by the complex of depreciation . . . Whenever
he thought of this at dinner,
he dug his heel into the carpet.

He had an army,
                    chariots of war,
but, as for her—
                    she owned a pair of lashes, eyes,
a star-resplendent
                    brow,
and a neck in curved surprise.

Когда они в носилках плыли,
то взгляды всех глазевших были
обращены,

              как по наитью,
не к фараону —

                    к Нефертити.

Был фараон угрюмым в ласке,
и допускал прямые грубости,
поскольку чуял хрупкость власти
в сравненьи с властью этой хрупкости.

А сфинксы

           медленно

                  выветривались,
и веры

          мертвенно

                  выверивались,
но сквозь идеи и событья,
сквозь все,

              в чем время обманулось,
тянулась шея Нефертити
и к нам сегодня дотянулась.
Она в мальчишечьем наброске,
и у монтажницы

                  на брошке.
Она кого-то очищает,
не приедаясь,

             не тускнея,
и кто-то снова ощущает

When on a litter shoulder-high they floated by,
then the gapers turned
their stares,
        intuitively,
not toward the pharaoh,
                but Nefertiti.

The pharaoh was rather grim in his affections,
and even allowed himself some crude gestures,
sensing the fragility of a potentate
when compared with the potency of fragility.

Slowly
      the sphinxes
                crumbled in the breeze,
and beliefs
          in deadly earnest
                    shed their faith,
but right through the ideas and events,
through all those things
                by which time is fooled,
Nefertiti's neck kept stretching out,
and, stretching, came into our days.
She figures now in some boy's drawing,
and on a working woman's
              brooch.
She acts to purify and liberate,
without palling
          or growing duller,
and again some person feels

неполноценность
                    рядом с нею.
Мы с вами часто вязнем в быте...
А Нефертити?
                    Нефертити
сквозь быт,
                сквозь битвы,
                            лица,
                                даты
все так же тянется куда-то.
Как ни крутите,
                ни вертите, —
но существует Нефертити.

his value depreciate
                              when set beside her.
We're often stuck in the daily rut . . .
And Nefertiti?
                    Nefertiti,
pushing out of the daily rut,
                    through battles,
                                        faces,
                                              dates,
still keeps on stretching somewhere.
Turn as you may,
                    and twist,
Nefertiti did exist.

1964.

Пришли иные времена

Пришли иные времена.
Взошли иные имена.

Они толкаются, бегут.
Они врагов себе пекут,
приносят неудобства
и вызывают злобства.

Ну а зато они — вожди,
и их девчонки ждут в дожди,
и, вглядываясь в сумрак,
украдкой брови слюнят.

А где же, где твои враги?
Хоть их опять искать беги...
Да вот они — радушно
кивают равнодушно.

А где твои девчонки, где?
Для их здоровья на дожде
опасно, не иначе, —
им надо внуков нянчить.

Украли всех твоих врагов.
Украли легкий стук шагов,
украли чей-то шепот...
Остался только опыт.

Но что же ты загоревал?
Скажи — ты сам не воровал,

Other Times

Other times have come.
Other names have risen.

They push and shove and run.
Making hard-baked enemies,
they create difficulties,
and give rise to spite and malice.

That's why they take the lead,
and girls wait for them in the rain,
and, peering through the dusk,
with furtive fingers wet their eyebrows.

Where are your foes, where are they?
You'd have trouble finding them again . . .
Ah, there they go, so blandly
cordial with their nodding heads.

Where are your girls, tell me where?
The rainy weather's dangerous
for their health, that's the matter—
baby-sitting, they'd rather stay at home.

All your enemies have been stolen.
Stolen, too, the tripping steps,
stolen the whispering of a voice . . .
Only the experience remains.

But why take it to heart and grieve?
Tell me—have you never thieved,

не заводя учета,
все это у кого-то?

Любая юность — воровство.
И в этом — жизни волшебство.
Ничто в ней не уходит,
а просто переходит.

Ты не завидуй. Будь мудрей,
Воров счастливых пожалей.
Ведь, как ни озоруют, —
их тоже обворуют.

Придут иные времена.
Взойдут иные имена.

and, failing to keep accounts,
stolen these things from someone else?

Youth is a form of thieving.
Therein lies all the magic of life.
Nothing passes entirely away,
but is simply a transition.

Be wiser then. Don't fall for envy.
Feel sorry for the lucky thieves.
However much they play the devil,
they'll end by being robbed themselves.

Other times will come.
Other names will rise.

1964.

Третья память

У всех такой бывает час:
тоска липучая пристанет
и, догола разоблачась,
вся жизнь бессмысленной предстанет.

Подступит мертвый хлад к нутру.
И, чтоб себя переупрямить,
как милосердную сестру,
зовем, почти бессильно, память.

Но в нас порой такая ночь,
такая в нас порой разруха,
когда не могут нам помочь
ни память сердца, ни рассудка.

Уходит блеск живой из глаз.
Движенья, речь — все помертвело.
Но третья память есть у нас,
и эта память — память тела.

Пусть ноги вспомнят наяву
и теплоту дорожной пыли,
и холодящую траву,
когда они босыми были.

Пусть вспомнит бережно щека,
как утешала после драки
доброшершавость языка
всепонимающей собаки.

The Third Memory

We all live through an hour like this,
when anguish sticks to you like glue
and, in stark nakedness exposed,
all life appears devoid of meaning.

A deadly chill will creep inside
and, to control that stubborn self,
we weakly summon memory
as we might call a nurse in aid.

In us at times there's such deep night,
at times in us such utter ruin,
that no memory of either reason
or heart can help us in our plight.

The gleam of life forsakes our eyes.
Movement and speech—these all are dead.
But a third memory we have—
the body's memory is this.

Then vividly let feet recall
the heat of dusty roads that scorched,
and fields of grass that used to chill
our soles when barefoot we tramped about.

And fondly let a cheek remember
the friendly understanding dog
that consoled us, bruised and battered
in a fight, with its good rough tongue.

Пусть виновато вспомнит лоб,
как на него, благословляя,
лег поцелуй, чуть слышно лег,
всю нежность матери являя.

Пусть вспомнит сладостно спина,
какая дремлющая нега
в душе земли затаена,
когда лежишь — глазами в небо.

Пусть вспомнят пальцы — хвою, рожь,
и дождь, почти неощутимый,
и дрожь воробышка, и дрожь
по нервной холке лошадиной.

Пусть вспомнят губы о губах.
В них лед и огонь. В них мрак со светом.
В них целый мир. Он весь пропах
и апельсинами и снегом...

Припомнишь — и проснется стыд.
Поймешь — порочить жизнь преступно.
И память тела возвратит
и память сердца, и рассудка.

И жизни скажешь ты: — Прости.
Я обвинял тебя вслепую.
Как тяжкий грех, мне отпусти
мою озлобленность тупую.

And feeling guilty, let your brow
remember how a kiss, in blessing,
touched it almost without sound,
a mother's tenderness expressing.

And let your back voluptuously
remember the drowsy languor biding
in earth's deep soul, as you lie there
with eyes devouring all the sky.

Let fingers feel the rye and conifers,
the almost impalpable rain,
a sparrow's shiver, and the quiver
down the nervous withers of a horse.

Let lips remember other lips.
Their ice and fire. Their gloom and glow.
The whole world in them. A world
all redolent of oranges and snow . . .

Shame will awake when you remember.
You'll grasp the crime of censuring life.
And body's memory will then restore
the memory of heart and reason.

And you will say to life: Forgive.
I used to blame you in my blindness.
As from a grievous sin, absolve
me of my raging bluntness.

И если надобно платить
за то, что этот мир прекрасен,
ценой жестокой — так и быть,
на эту плату я согласен.

Но и превратности в судьбе,
но и удары и утраты,
жизнь, за прекрасное в тебе —
такая ли большая плата?!

And if we are obliged to pay
a savage price because this world
is beautiful—all right, I'll say,
I shall consent to pay the price.

But, life, are all the stringencies
of fate, the losses, sudden blows,
so great a price for me to pay
for all the beauty you contain?!

1964

Мертвая рука прошлого

Кое-кто живет еще по-старому,
в новое всадить пытаясь нож.
Кое-кто глядит по-сталински,
сумрачно косясь на молодежь.
Кое-кто, еще не укротившийся,
оттянуть ее пытаясь вниз,
яростно за стрелку уцепившийся
на часах истории повис.
Кое-кто в бессильной злобе мается.
Что-же, знаю я наверняка,
что рука труднее разжимается,
если это мертвая рука.

Мертвая рука прошлого —
крепко ты еще вцепилась в нас.
Мертвая рука прошлого —
ничего без боя не отдаст.
Мертвая рука прошлого —
ты не победишь живых.
Мертвая рука прошлого —
вырвемся из пальцев твоих.
Мертвая рука прошлого —
пусть борьба с тобою тяжка.
Мертвая рука прошлого —
все-таки ты — мертвая душа.

The Dead Hand of The Past

Someone is still living as of old,
attempting to knife whatever's new.
Someone still glares in the Stalin manner,
looking at young men askance.
Someone still untamed and restless
fiercely grips the hour hand
and, in striving to drag it down,
hangs on to history's clock.
Someone pines in impotent anger.
That may be, but I for certain know
it's harder to unclench a fist
if the fist is that of a dead hand.

Dead hand of the past,
your grip on us is still quite strong.
The dead hand of the past
will yield nought without a struggle.
Dead hand of the past,
you will not destroy the living.
Dead hand of the past,
we'll break your fingers' hold.
Dead hand of the past,
let it be a hard fight between us.
Dead hand of the past,
you're a dead hand to the last.

V. The City of "Yes" and the City of "No"

"My poetry, like Cinderella . . .
washes the soiled linen of this age."

Женщина и море

Над морем —
               молнии.
Из глубины
взмывают мордами
                  к ним
                  лобаны.
Нас в лодке пятеро.
За пядью —
            пядь.
А море спятило,
                относит вспять.

Доцентик химии
под ливнем плещущим
так прячет
            хилые
свои плечики.
Король пинг-понга
в техасских джинсах
вдруг,
        как поповна,
крестясь,
ложится.
Культурник Миша
дрожит,
          как мышь.
Где его мышцы?
Что толку с мышц?!
Все смотрят жертвенно,
держась за сердце...

The Woman and the Sea

Flashes of lightning
                    light the sea.
Out of the depths
the mullets raise
                    their gullets of foam
towards them.
There were five of us in the boat.
Hand over hand
                    we advance.
But the sea then beat a retreat,
                                sweeping us back.
Under the lashing shower,
the chemistry lecturer
huddles,
        hiding
his skinny shoulders.
The ping pong king
in his Texas jeans
suddenly
        lies down,
fervently blessing himself,
like any parish priest's wife.
Misha the gymnast
trembles
        like a mouse.
Where are his biceps?
What good his muscles here?
All three gape like scapegoats,
each clutching at his heart . . .

И вдруг —
                та женщина
на весла села!
И вот над веслами,
над кашей чертовой
возникли волосы,
как факел черный!
Вошла ей в душу
игра —
игла.
Рыбачкой дюжей
она гребла.
Гребла загадка
для волн
                и нас,
вся —
                из загара
и рыжих глаз!
Ей,
        медной,
        мокрой,
простой,
как Маугли,
                    и мало —
молний!
и моря —
мало!

Всего, что било,
всего, что мяло,
ей мало было!

But all of a sudden
                    that woman
sat down to the oars!
And above the oars then,
above the devil's own brew,
a mass of hair loomed
like a black torch!
And the sport of it,
needle-like, bit
deep into her soul.
Like a sturdy fisherman,
she rowed on.
Rowed on, an enigma
to the waves
                    and to us,
in appearance
                    all tan
and reddish eyes!
For her,
        bronzed,
        drenched,
simple
        as Mowgli,
the lightning's
                    not too big!
The sea's
        not too big!

All that was battering us,
All that was crumpling us,
was not too big for her!

да!

    мало!

        мало!

Уже не барышней,

сопя подчеркнуто,

доцентик

          баночкой

полез вычерпывать.

Король пинг-понга

под рев неистовый

вдруг стал

          приподнято

свой «рок» насвистывать.

Культурник вспомнил,

что он —

          мужчина...

Всех,

       с морем в споре,

она

      учила!

А море бухало

о буты

       бухты.

Мы были

         будто

бунт

       против бунта!

No!

      not too big!

                not too big!

Girlish no longer,
sniffling emphatically,
the lecturer
          now crawled
to bail out with a can.
To the horrendous howling,
the ping-pong king
of a sudden began,
                raising his voice,
to whistle his "rock and roll."
The gymnast remembered
he was
      a man.

She lessoned
          us all,
who scuffled
          with the sea!
And the seas kept battering
against the rocks
             of the bay.
And we seemed
          to be
in revolt
        against a rebellion!

Летя сквозь волны,
расставшись с жестами,
мы были —

                    воины,
и вождь наш —

                    женщина!

В любые трудности,
в любые сложности,
когда по трусости
мы станем ежиться, —
на все пошедшие,
сильны,

            смешливы,
напомнят женщины,
что мы —

            мужчины!
Всего, что мяло
и что ломало,
нам станет мало!
Да —

        мало!

                мало!

Flying through the waves,
our gestures left behind,
we now
            were warriors,
and a woman
                    was our chief!

In moments of stress,
complication and distress,
when out of cowardice,
we begin to squirm,
then women who dare all,
who are strong,
                    and like to laugh,
will remind us
that we
        are men!
All that was crumpling us,
all that was battering us,
will prove not too big!
No!
    not too big!
                    not too big!

1962

Страхи

Умирают в России страхи,
словно призраки прежних лет,
лишь на паперти, как старухи,
кое-где еще просят на хлеб.

Я их помню во власти и силе
при дворе торжествующей лжи.
Страхи всюду, как тени, скользили,
проникали во все этажи.

Потихоньку людей приручали
и на все налагали печать:
где молчать бы — кричать приучали,
и молчать — где бы надо кричать.

Это стало сегодня далеким.
Даже странно и вспомнить теперь
тайный страх перед чьим-то доносом,
тайный страх перед стуком в дверь.

Ну, а страх говорить с иностранцем?
С иностранцем-то что, а с женой?
Ну, а страх беспредельный — остаться
после маршей вдвоем с тишиной?

Не боялись мы строить в метели,
уходить под снарядами в бой,
но боялись порою смертельно
разговаривать сами с собой.

Fears

Fears are dying out in Russia
like the ghosts of bygone years,
and only like old women, here and there,
they still beg for alms on the steps of a church.

But I remember them in their strength and power
at the court of triumphing falsehood.
Like shadows, fears crept in everywhere,
and penetrated to every floor.

Gradually, they made people subservient,
and set their seal upon all things:
they taught us to shout when we should have kept silent,
and to shut our mouths when we had need to shout.

Today all this has become remote.
It's strange even to recall nowadays
the secret fear of being denounced,
the secret fear of a knock at the door.

And what of the fear of speaking to a foreigner?
A foreigner's one thing, but what of speaking to one's wife?
And what of the boundless fear of remaining
alone with silence after the brass bands have stopped?

We were not afraid of building in the blizzard,
or of going into battle while shells exploded,
but at times we were mortally afraid
of even talking to ourselves.

Нас не сбили и не растлили;
и недаром сейчас во врагах
победившая страхи Россия
еще больший рождает страх!

Я хочу, чтоб людьми овладели
страх кого-то судить без суда,
страх неправдой унизить идеи,
страх неправдой возвысить себя,

страх к другим оставаться бесстрастным,
если кто-то в беде и тоске,
страх отчаянный быть не бесстрашным
на холсте и чертежной доске.

И когда я пишу эти строки
и порою невольно спешу,
то пишу их в единственном страхе,
что не в полную силу пишу...

We were not corrupted or led astray;
and Russia, having conquered her fears,
gives rise—not without reason—to even
greater fear among her enemies!

I wish that men were possessed of the fear
of condemning a man without proper trial,
the fear of debasing ideas by means of untruth,
the fear of exalting oneself by means of untruth,

the fear of remaining indifferent to others,
when someone is in trouble or depressed,
the desperate fear of not being fearless
when painting on a canvas or drafting a sketch.

And as I write these lines—
and I am in too great a haste at times—
I have only one fear when writing them:
the fear of not writing with all my power.

Песня надсмотрщиков

Мы — надсмотрщики,
мы —
            твои ножки,
                        трон.
При виде нас
            морщится
брезгливо
            фараон.
А что он без нас?
Без наших глаз?
Без наших глоток?
Без наших плеток?
Плетка —
            лекарство,
хотя она не мед.
Основа государства —
надсмотр,
надсмотр.
Народ без назидания
работать бы не смог.
Основа созиданья —
надсмотр,
            надсмотр.
И воины, раскиснув,
бежали бы, как сброд.
Основа героизма —
надсмотр,
            надсмотр.
Опасны, кто задумчивы.
Всех мыслящих —
            к закланью.

The Song of the Overseers

We are the overseers.
We are
          your legs,
                    O throne.
At the sight of us
                    the Pharaoh
squeamishly
                    turns up his nose.
But what is he without us?
Without our eyes?
Without our throats?
Without our whips?
The lash
          is good medicine,
though not as sweet as honey.
The foundation of the state—
is overseeing,
                    overseeing.
Without exhortation, the people
could not work.
The basis of creation
is overseeing,
                    overseeing.
And warriors, turned sour,
would scatter like a rabble.
The foundation of heroism
is overseeing,
                    overseeing.
Thoughtful men are dangerous.
All who think
                    must be immolated.

Надсмотр за душами
важней,
чем за телами.
Вы что-то загалдели?
Вы снова за нытье?
Свободы захотели?
А разве нет ее?!
(И звучат не слишком бодро
голоса:
          «Есть!
                    Есть!» —
то ли есть у них свобода,
то ли хочется им есть.)
Мы —
                    надсмотрщики.
Мы гуманно грубые.
Мы вас бьем не до смерти,
для вашей пользы, глупые.
Плетками
          по черным
                    спинам
рубя,
внушаем:
          «Почетна
работа
          раба».
Что о свободе грезить?
Имеете вы, дурни,
свободу —

It is more important to oversee
souls
        than bodies.
You're shouting again?
You're complaining again?
Is it freedom you want?
But don't you already have it?!
(And not-too-confident voices
reply:
        "We have it!
                        We have it!"
but have they freedom
or do they want to eat?)
We are
        the overseers.
We are humanely brutal.
We don't thrash you to death,
we lash you for your own good, you dolts.
Welting
        black
                backs
with our whips,
we suggest:
                "The work
a slave does
            is honorable."
Why dream of freedom?
Fools, you have
the freedom—

                    сколько влезет
молчать,
                    о чем вы думаете.
Мы — надсмотрщики.
С нас тоже
                    пот ручьем.
Рабы,
        вы нас не можете
упрекнуть
                    ни в чем.
Мы смотрим настороженно.
Мы псы —
                    лишь без намордников.
Но ведь и мы,
                    надсмотрщики, —
рабы других надсмотрщиков.
И над рабами стонущими,
раб Амона он —
надсмотрщик всех надсмотрщиков,
наш бедный фараон...

                        as much as you can take,
to be silent
                about what you're thinking.
We are the overseers.
We also sweat
                    in streams.
Slaves,
        there's no reproach
you can make
                    against us.
Our eyes are watchful.
We're hounds—
                    but have no muzzles.
But we,
        the overseers,
are slaves to other overseers.
And above the groaning slaves
stands Amon's slave—
the overseer of all overseers,
our poor Pharaoh . . .

1965

"Да" и "Нет"

(Из стихов о любви)

Я, как поезд,

что мечется столько уж лет

между городом «Да»

и городом «Нет».

Мои нервы натянуты,

как провода,

между городом «Нет»

и городом «Да».

Нет любви в этом городе «Нет».

Он похож

на обитый тоской кабинет.

По утрам

натирают в нем желчью паркет.

В нем насупился замкнуто

каждый предмет.

В нем диваны —

из фальши,

в нем стены —

из бед.

Черта с два

в нем получишь ты

добрый совет,

или, скажем, букет,

или просто привет.

Пишмашинки стучат

под копирку ответ:

«Нет-нет-нет...

нет-нет-нет...

нет-нет-нет...»

А когда

совершенно погасится свет,

"Yes" and "No"

FROM VERSES ABOUT LOVE

I'm like a train
              that's been shuttling for years
between the city of "Yes"
                      and the city of "No."
My nerves strain,
                  like the telegraph wires,
between the city of "No"
                      and the city of "Yes."
There's no love in this city of "No."
It resembles
          a room upholstered with anguish.
There, in the morning,
                      they polish the parquet with bile.
Each object there
                  sullenly scowls.
The sofas
        are of spurious material.
The walls—
          of misfortune.
What chance
          of your receiving good counsel,
or, let's say, a bouquet
                      or even a welcome.
All the answer you get
                      is a carbon copy:
"No-no-no . . .
          No-no-no . . .
                      No-no-no . . ."
And when
        the light's completely switched off,

начинают в нем призраки
                мрачный балет.
Черта с два —
                хоть подохни! —
                достанешь билет,
чтоб уехать
                из черного города «Нет»...
Ну, а в городе «Да»
                жизнь, как песня дрозда.
Этот город без стен,
                он подобье гнезда.
В руки просится с неба
                любая звезда,
просят губы любые
                твоих
                без стыда,
бормоча еле слышно:
                «А.... все ерунда!», —
и сорвать себя просит,
                дразня,
                резеда,
и, мыча,
                молоко предлагают
                стада,
и ни в ком подозрения
                нет ни следа,
и, куда ты захочешь,
                мгновенно туда
унесут поезда,
                самолеты,
                суда,

ghosts in that room
                    dance a somber ballet.
What chance—
             try as you may—
                          of getting a ticket
to travel away
            from the black city of "No" . . .
But in the city of "Yes,"
                    life's like the song of a thrush.
No walls in this city—
                  it looks like a nest.
Any star of the city
                just begs to fall in your hands;
lips, any lips,
           unashamed, just ask for your lips,
barely mumbling:
             "Ah, what nonsense this!"
and teasingly the mignonette
                        begs you
                              to pluck it,
and, lowing,
         the herds
                 offer their milk,
and no trace of suspicion
                     lurks in man,
and wherever you might want to go,
                             instantly
the trains,
       the planes,
               the ships will take you there.

и, журча,

             как года,

             чуть лепечет вода:

«Да-да-да...

             да-да-да...

             да-да-да...»

Только скучно,

             по правде сказать,

             иногда,

что дается мне столько

             почти без труда

в разноцветно светящемся

             городе «Да»...

Пусть уж лучше мечусь

             до конца моих лет

между городом «Да»

             и городом «Нет»!

Пусть уж нервы натянуты,

             как провода,

между городом «Нет»

             и городом «Да»!

And babbling
          like the years,
                    the water just lisps:
"Yes-yes-yes . . .
               Yes-yes-yes . . .
                         Yes-yes-yes . . ."
It's tedious though,
               truth to tell,
                    what I manage to do
at times
          without straining at all
in the multicolored,
               brightly-lit
                    city of "Yes" . . .
I'd do better to shuttle
                    to the end of my years
between the city of "Yes"
                    and the city of "No"!
Let my nerves strain,
                    like the telegraph wires,
between the city of "No"
                    and the city of "Yes."

Золушка

Моя поэзия,
                           как Золушка,
забыв про самое свое,
стирает каждый день,
                           чуть зорюшка,
эпохи грязное белье.
Покуда падчерица пачкается,
чумаза,
              словно нетопырь,
наманикюренные пальчики
девицы сушат врастопыр.
Да,
         жизнь ее порою тошная.
Да,
         ей не сладко понимать,
что пахнет луком и картошкою,
а не шанелью номер пять.
Лишь иногда за все ей воздано —
посуды выдраив навал,
она спешит,
                           воздушней воздуха,
белее белого,
                           на бал!
И феей,
              а не замарашкою,
с лукавой магией в зрачках
она,
         дразня и завораживая,
идет в хрустальных башмачках.
Но бьют часы,
                           и снова мучиться,

Cinderella

My poetry,
        like Cinderella,
forgetting its own essential tasks,
washes, as from dawn's first glimmer,
                        every day,
the soiled linen of this age.
While the step-daughter does the dirty work—
that smudge-face,
                dusky as a bat—
the young ladies dry their nail-polish,
holding their fingers spread apart.
Yes,
      her life is sickening at times.
Yes,
      it's not sweet for her to know
the smell of onion and potato
rather than the scent of Chanel No. 5.
Only now and then is all her toil rewarded
and, after reducing a pile of dirty dishes,
she hastens,
           lighter than the air,
whiter than any white,
                to a grand ball!
And like a Fey,
           no smudge-face now,
a cunning glint of magic in her eyes,
she,
teasing and bewitching,
                 trips along in crystal shoes.
But then midnight strikes
              and, hard-pressed again,

стирать,

и штопать,

и скрести

она бежит,

бежит из музыки,

бежит,

бежит из красоты.

И до рассвета ночью позднею

она,

усталая,

не спит

и, на коленках с тряпкой ползая,

полы истории скоблит.

В альковах сладко спят наследницы,

а замарашке —

как ей быть?! —

ведь если так полы наслежены,

кому-то надо же их мыть.

Она их трет и трет,

не ленится,

а где-то,

словно светлячок,

переливается на лестнице

забытый ею башмачок...

she scampers back,
                    running out of the music,
running,
          running out of beauty,
to launder,
           darn,
                  and sweep.
And late into the night, till dawn,
the exhausted girl
                    can find
                            no sleep
and, crawling on her knees,
scrubs the floors of history.
The heiresses drowse sweetly in their alcoves;
and as for smudge-face—
                        what is she to do?
For, if the floors are all that soiled,
somebody must wash them, that is so!
No lazybones, she scrubs and scrubs
                                the floors,
and somewhere,
               like a glow-worm,
the shoe she has forgotten
stands sparkling on the stair . . .

Вздох

Он замкнут,

старый друг мой,

замкнут.

Он внутрь себя собою загнан.

Закрыл он, будто бы колодец,

глубины темные тоски,

и мысли в крышку ту колотят

и разбивают кулаки.

Он этих мыслей не расскажет,

он их не выплачет навзрыд,

и все в нем глухо нарастает,

и я боюсь,

что будет взрыв.

Но взрыва нет,

а только вздох,

и вздох —

как слезы бабьи в стог,

как моря судорожный всхлип

у мокрых сумеречных глыб.

Я раньше был открыт-открыт,

ни в чем себя не сдерживал,

за что и был судьбой отбрит,

как женщиной насмешливой.

И я устал.

Я замкнут стал.

Я доверяться перестал.

Себя порою во хмелю

почти на взрыве я ловлю,

но взрыва нет,

а только вздох,

The Sigh

He's withdrawn,
　　　　　my old friend,
　　　　　withdrawn.
He's driven himself inside.
As in a well, he's shut himself in
deep in his nostalgia,
and his thoughts hammer against that lid,
and his fists smash against it.
He will not tell you what he's thinking,
nor sob out these thoughts brokenly,
and sullenly it all piles up within him,
and I fear
　　　　　an explosion.
But no explosion comes,
　　　　　　　　only a sigh,
and that sigh's
　　　　　like a woman weeping in the hay,
like the sea's shuddering gasp
as it drenches the rocks at dusk.
I was like an open book before,
and never held back at all,
and, for this, fate rebuffed me
like a disdainful woman.
And now I'm tired.
　　　　　　　I've become shut in.
I've ceased to trust.
At times, when drinking,
I almost catch myself exploding.
But no explosion comes,
　　　　　　　only a sigh,

и вздох —

                   как слезы бабьи в стог,
как моря судорожный всхлип
у мокрых сумеречных глыб.

Мой старый друг,

                   мой нелюдим,
давай, как прежде, посидим,
давай по чарочке нальемъ,
давай вздохнем —

                   уже вдвоем...

and the sigh's
                like a woman weeping in the hay,
like the seas's shuddering gasp
as it drenches the rocks at dusk.

My old, my unsociable
                        friend,
let us sit down as we used to do,
let's fill a glass each,
let us sigh—
                this time together.

Итальянские слезы

Возле Братска, в поселке Анзёба
плакал рыжий хмельной кладовщик.
Это страшно всегда до озноба,
если плачет не баба — мужик.

И, корежась нечеловечьи,
удержаться старалось лицо,
но тряслись неподвластные плечи,
а из глаз все лило и лило.

Все выкладывал он до крохи,
как под Минском, он был окружен,
как по дальней железной дороге
был отправлен в Италию он.

«Но лопата — пойми! — не копала
в огражденной от всех полосе,
а роса на шоссе проступала,
понимаешь — роса на шоссе!

И однажды с корзиночкой мимо
итальянка девчушечка шла,
и что люди голодные, мигом,
будто русской была, поняла.

Востроносая, словно грачонок,
протянула какой-то их фрукт
из своих семилетних ручонок,
как из бабьих жалетельных рук.

Italian Tears

In the village of Anzeba, close to Bratsk,
a red-haired storekeeper was weeping drunkenly.
A terrible thing, it always gives me the shivers,
to see a man, not a woman, sobbing.

Inhumanly straining his face,
the man tried to look composed,
but his meager shoulders were shaking,
and from his eyes tears poured and poured.

To the last drop he was spilling it out;
how he had been surrounded near Minsk,
and had then been packed off by long
distance rail to Italy far away.

"You'll understand," he said, "my spade would not dig
in the sector fenced off from all,
and on the highway we could see the dew rise,
you understand, the dew on the highway!

"And with a basket one day a child,
An Italian girl, was passing by,
and, as if she were Russian, she grasped at once
there were hungry men behind that fence.

"She was beak-nosed like a young rook,
and she held out an Italian fruit to us,
holding it in her seven-year-old little hands
that were like the hands of a compassionate woman.

Ну, а этим фашистам проклятым —
что им дети, что люди кругом!
И солдат ее вдарил прикладом,
и вдобавок еще — сапогом.

И упала, раскинувши руки,
и лежала она на шоссе,
и заплакала горько, по-русски,
так, что сразу мы поняли все.

Сколько наша братва отстрадала,
оттерпела от дома вдали,
но, чтоб эта девчушка рыдала,
мы уже потерпеть не могли.

И овчарок, солдат — мы в лопаты,
рассекая их сучьи хрящи,
ну, а после уже — в автоматы:
оказались они хороши.

И свобода нам хлынула в горло,
и, вертлявая, точно юла,
к партизанам их тамошним в горы
та девчушечка нас повела.

Были там и рабочие парни,
и крестьяне — и я пободрел.
Был священник — по-ихнему «падре»...
Так что к богу я, брат, подобрел.

"But, as for those damned Fascists—
what did they care for children or people!
A guard struck her with a rifle butt,
and booted her hard into the bargain.

"And she fell with arms flung out,
and lay sprawling on the highway,
and bitterly she began to sob in Russian,
and we understood it all at once.

"Though our band of brothers had gone through much,
and suffered many trials so far from home,
yet we could stand it no longer
to hear that little girl sobbing.

"And with spades we attacked the dogs and the guards,
splitting their bitchy cartileges,
and then we took to the automatics:
they did their work well.

"And freedom gushed to our throats,
and as elusive as a spinning top,
that little girl led us into the mountains
to join the Italian partisans there.

"Among them were also working lads,
and peasants too—and I took courage.
Likewise there was a priest—'*padre*' they called him . . .
and thus it was, brother, I came nearer to God.

Мы делили затяжки, и пули,
и любой сокровенный секрет,
и порою, ей-богу, я путал,
кто был русский в отряде, кто нет.

Что оливы, браток, что березы —
это, в общем, почти все равно.
Итальянские, русские слезы
и любые — все это одно...»

«А потом?» — «А потом при оружьи
мы входили под музыку в Рим.
Гладиолусы плюхались в лужи,
и шагали мы прямо по ним.

Развевался и флаг партизанский,
и английский, как миленький, был,
и зебрастый американский —
лишь про нашенский Рим позабыл.

Но один старичишка у храма
подошел и по-русски сказал:
«Я шофер из посольства Сиама,
а посол был фашист — он сбежал.

Эмигрант я, но родину помню...
Здесь он рядом — тот брошенный дом.
Флаг, смотрите-ка, — алое поле,
только лев затесался на нем».

"We shared the delays and the bullets,
all of our innermost secrets,
and at times, I swear, I couldn't tell
a Russian from an Italian in that detachment.

"Olive tree or birch tree, brother,
it was almost all the same.
Italian tears or Russian tears
or other tears—it was all the same . . ."

"And then?"—"And then, bearing arms,
we entered Rome to the sound of music.
Gladioli showered down into the puddles
and we trampled on them as we marched.

"The Partisan flag was also fluttering,
and endearingly the Union Jack was there,
and also the Stars and Stripes—
but Rome had forgotten all about our flag.

"But next to a church an elderly man
came up to us and said in Russian:
'I'm a chauffeur at the Embassy of Siam,
and our Fascist ambassador took to his heels.

" 'Though an emigrant, I remembered my land . . .
It's close by, the house I abandoned.
Just look at that flag—a field of crimson,
but somehow a lion has intruded upon it.'

И тогда, не смущаясь нимало,
финкарями спороли мы льва,
но чего-то еще не хватало —
мы не поняли даже сперва.

А чернявый грачонок Мария
(пусть простит ей сиамский посол!)
хвать-ка ножницы из барберии,
Да и шварк! — от юбчонки подол.

И чего-то она верещала,
улыбалась — хитрехонько так,
и чего-то она вырезала,
а потом нашивала на флаг.

И взлетел — аж глаза стали мокнуть
у братвы загрубелой, лютой
красный флаг, а на нем серп и молот
из юбчонки девчушечки той...»

«А потом?» Похмурел он, запнувшись,
дернул спирта под сливовый джем,
а лицо было в детских веснушках
и в морщинах — недетских совсем.

«А потом через Каспий мы плыли.
Обнимались и в пляс на борту!
Мы героями вроде как были,
но героями — лишь до Баку.

"And then, in no way embarrassed,
with our knives we ripped off the lion,
but something was still missing—
we didn't quite get it at first.

"And Maria, that black little rook,
(may the Siamese Ambassador forgive her!)
snatched a pair of scissors from a barber's,
and snipped off the hem of her skirt.

"And chirping out some words,
with a sly smile on her face,
she kept cutting bits and pieces,
and then sewing them onto the flag.

"And then it flew high—bringing tears
to the eyes of that rough fighting band—
that flag with a hammer and sickle upon it,
fashioned from the skirt of the little girl.

"What then?" He frowned and stammered, and took
a swig of crude liquor and a mouthful of plum jam,
while his face was all freckled like a child's,
and wrinkled too—but the wrinkles weren't those of a child.

"And then we were crossing the Caspian.
We hugged each other and danced on board!
We were some kind of heroes,
but heroes only until we reached Baku.

Гладиолусами не встречали,
а встречали, браток, при штыках.
И угрюмо овчарки ворчали
на отечественных поводках.

Конвоиров безусые лица
с подозреньем смотрели на нас,
и кричали мальчишки нам «фрицы!»,
так, что слезы вставали у глаз.

Весь в прыщах, лейтенант-необстрелок
в форме новенькой — так его мать! —
нам спокойно сказал: «Без истерик!»
и добавил: «Оружие — сдать».

И солдатики нас по-пастушьи
привели, как овец сосчитав,
к так знакомой колючей подружке
в так знакомых железных цветах.

И куда ты негаданно делась
в нашей собственной кровной стране,
партизанская прежняя смелость?
Или, может, приснилась во сне?

Опустили мы головы низко
и оружие сдали легко.
До Италии было неблизко,
А до дому совсем далеко.

"We were not greeted with gladioli,
but were met with fixed bayonets, brother.
And sullenly the police dogs growled
as we were carted away.

"The clean-shaven faces of our convoy guards
stared with suspicion at us,
and small boys yelled out: 'Down with the Fritzes!'
And this made tears well up to our eyes.

"A pimply lieutenant, who hadn't seen fire,
all decked out in a new uniform—may he rot!
addressed us calmly: 'No hysteria now!'
and he added: 'Give up your arms!'

And like shepherds, the guards
counted us like sheep and then drove us along
to the 'barbed-wire' retreat we knew so well,
all burgeoning with familiar iron flowers.

"And where had you so inexplicably vanished
in the land of our own flesh-and-blood,
that partisan valor of former days?
Or, perhaps, it had been only a dream.

"We hung our heads low,
and easily surrendered our arms.
Now Italy was not at all near,
and it was a long way from home.

Я, кидая оружье и шмотки,
под рубашкою спрятал тот флаг,
но его отобрали при шмоне:
«Недостоин... — сказали. — Ты враг...»

И лежал на оружье безмолвном,
что досталось нам в битве святой
красный флаг, а на нем серп и молот
из юбчонки девчушечки той...»

«А потом?» Усмехнулся он желчно,
после спирту еще пропустил,
да и ложкой комкастого джема,
искривившись, его подсластил.

Вновь лицо он сдержал через силу
и не знал — его спрятать куда:
«А — не стоит... Что было — то было,
только б не было так никогда...

Завтра рано вставать мне — работа...
Ну, а будешь в Италии ты:
где-то в городе Монте-Ротонда
там живут партизаны-браты.

И Мария — вся в черных колечках,
а быть может, в седых — столько лет!
Передай, если помнит, конечно,
ей от рыжего Вани привет.

"Throwing down my arms and ragged belongings,
I tucked that flag under my shirt;
but they took it away when they frisked me.
'You're no good,' they said. 'You're an enemy.'

"And there it lay on our heaped speechless arms,
that red flag we had gained in the sacred battle
we'd waged, and upon it was the hammer and sickle
that had been made from the little girl's skirt . . ."

"And what then?" He gave a jaundiced smile,
took another gulp of crude liquor
and, grimacing, followed it up
with a spoonful of chunky plum jam.

Again he made an effort to look composed,
not knowing where to hide his face:
"Ah, it's not worth it . . . What's done is done,
but may it never happen again. . . .

"I must get up early tomorrow—there's work to do . . .
But if you ever find yourself in Italy:
somewhere in the town of Monte Rotondo
you'll come across our brother-partisans living there.

"And Maria—with all her black ringlets,
and even gray ones, maybe—many years have passed.
Give her my greetings, if she remembers of course,
greetings from red-haired Vanya.

Ну не надо про лагерь, понятно.
Как сказал, что прошло — то прошло.
Ты скажи им — им будет приятно —
в общем, Ваня живет хорошо...»

...Ваня, все же я в Монте-Ротонде
побывал, как просил меня ты.
Там крестьянин, шофер и ремонтник
обнимали меня, как браты.

Я не видел синьоры Марии,
только просто зашел в ее дом,
и смотрели твои голубые
с фотографии — рядом с Христом.

Меня спрашивали и крестьяне
и священник — весь белый, как снег:
«Как там Ванья?» «Как Ванья?» «Как Ванья?»
и вздыхали: «Такой человек!»

Партизаны стояли рядами —
столько их для расспросов пришло,
и твердил я, скрывая рыданья:
«В общем, Ваня живет хорошо...»

Были мы ни пьяны, ни тверезы,
просто пели и пили вино.
Итальянские, русские слезы
и любые — все это одно.

"Don't tell her about the camp, you understand.
As I said, what's done is done.
But tell them—they'll be glad to hear it—
that Vanya's living well, on the whole . . ."

. . . Vanya, all the same, I did go to Monte
Rotondo, as you had asked me to do.
The peasant, the chauffer and the fitter,
embraced me like a brother there.

I did not see signora Maria,
but simply paid a call to her house,
and there I saw your blue eyes looking down
from a photograph beside the image of Christ.

I was asked by the peasants and
by the priest—all white as snow:
"How's Vanya?" "How's Vanya?" "How's Vanya?"
and they said with a sigh, "What a man!"

The partisans stood in ranks—
so many had come to ask questions,
and I kept affirming, restraining my sobs:
"Your Vanya's living fairly well, on the whole . . ."

We were neither too drunk, nor too sober—
all we did was to sing and drink wine.
Italian tears or Russian tears
or any other tears—are very much the same.

Что ж ты плачешь, опять наливая,
что ж ты цедишь: «А, все это блажь!»
Тебя помнит Италия, Ваня,
и запомнит Россия — не плачь!

Why are you weeping, gulping liquor again,
Why do you grind out: "Ah, it's only a fancy!"
Italy still remembers you, Vanya,
and Russia will recall you too—so don't weep!

Западные киновпечатления

Прочь акатоне,

                  прочь пеонов —

айда на фильмы про шпионов!

Что Гамлет!

              или Хиросима!

Страданья —

          это некрасиво.

Красиво —

          чью-то ручку чмокнуть,

и вдруг —

          наручник на нее.

Красиво —

          выследить и чпокнуть.

Не жизнь — малина,

          ё-моё!

Что толку шумным быть поэтом,

какая в этом благодать!

А вот бесшумным пистолетом

полезней,

        право,

            обладать!

Чекист сибирский

           Лев Огрехов

вербует водкой бедных греков

и разбивается на части,

вооруженный до зубов,

внезапно выпрыгнув из пасти

рекламы пасты для зубов.

Impressions of the Western Cinema

To hell with *Accatone*
                    and films about peons—
let's go and watch spy thrillers!
What's Hamlet
                    or Hiroshima!
To see people suffer,
                    isn't very handsome.
It's handsome
                    to kiss a lady's hand
and then, of a sudden,
                    snap a handcuff on her.
It's handsome
                    to tail a man and flatten him out.
It's not life—it's a bowl of cherries,
                    nothing better!
What's the point of being a celebrated poet,
what bliss is there in that!
It's far more practical to own
a pistol
        with a silencer,
                    that's right!
Lev Ogrekhov,
                    of the Siberian Cheka,
with vodka's help recruits poor Greeks
and, armed to the teeth,
splits into fragments,
as he suddenly leaps from the jaws
of an ad for toothpaste.

С мешком резиновым тротила
американец Джон О'Нил,
напялив шкуру крокодила,
переплывает ночью Нил.

Следя за тайнами красавиц,
шпион китайский —

                тощий Ван,
насквозь пружинами пронзаясь,
ложится доблестно в диван.

И там, страдая,

                вместо: «Мама...»
он грустно шепчет:

                «Мяу... Мяу...»
И над всеми,

            как над плебсом,
ведя себя с английским блеском,
целует девочек взасос
Джеймс Бонд —

            шпион, Иисус Христос!

С ума схожу.

           Себя же боязно.
Быть может, я и сам шпион!
Я скручен лентами шпионскими,
как змеями —

           Лаокоон.

Вот к вам приходит друг с бутылкой.
Не слишком кажется ли пылкой

With a rubber bag of T.N.T.,
the American John O'Neill,
pulling on a crocodile hide,
swims at night across the Nile.

Spying on beautiful women's secrets,
the Chinese agent—
                    gaunt Li Van—
spiking himself on the springs,
crawls bravely inside a divan.

And suffering there,
                    instead of "Mama" . . .
he sadly whispers:
                    "Mao . . . Mao . . ."
And there,
          above the common herd,
carrying himself with English smartness,
he kisses the girls in one long breath,
this man James Bond—
                    the secret agent, Jesus Christ!

I'm going off my rocker.
                    I'm frightened of myself.
Perhaps I am a secret agent too?
In the coils of espionage I'm caught
as Laocoön
          was coiled in snakes.

A friend with a bottle calls to see you,
His words—do they strike you

вам речь его?

               Воркует бас...

А может, он вербует вас?!

Вот ночью женщина в постели
вам что-то шепчет еле-еле.
В ее глазах такая качка...
А может быть, она стукачка?!

Ваш дядя —

          самых честных правил —
купил тройной одеколон.
Он вас подумать не заставил,
что он в душе —

             тройной шпион?!

Вот мира этого Бербанк!
Шпикам на радость мокроносым
скрестил он розу с микрофоном
и положил мильончик в банк.
Но, кстати, знайте,

            что пионы
уже давным-давно —

             шпионы.

Мне снится мир под мрачным сводом,
где завербована луна,
где городам и пароходам
дают шпионов имена.

as too persuasive?
                                A cooing bass . . .
Maybe he's seeking your cooperation?

There, in bed at night, a woman
keeps whispering words you can barely hear.
Her eyes are rolling . . .
But, maybe, she's just a squealer?

Your uncle—
                    strict in his demeanor—
bought some triple-strong cologne.
He did not force you to believe
that, in his heart, he was—
                                a triple agent!

There he is, the Burbank of this world!
To the delight of sniveling gumshoes,
he crossed a rose with a microphone,
and dumped a million in his bank.
But, incidentally, you should know

                                that peonies
have been secret agents—
                                since long ago.

I dream of a world beneath a dark night sky
in which the moon has been recruited,
in which ships and cities have been named
after notorious secret agents.

Спешат шпионы-делегаты
на мировой шпионский съезд.
Висят призывные плакаты:
«Кто не шпионит — тот не ест».

И тысячи живых шпионов,
как совесть наций, честь и суд,
букеты розо-микрофонов
к шпионам бронзовым несут...

Довольно!
          Этот сон кошмарен.
Он с ядом,
            этот жуткий джем.
Я, может, не совсем нормален,
но ненормален не совсем.

Реклама,
        брось шипеть неоном!
В моем понятии простом
шпион останется шпионом,
Христос останется Христом.

The spy delegates are in great haste
to attend the world congress of secret agents.
There they hang, the welcoming posters!
"He shall not eat, who is no spy."

And to spies in monumental bronze
thousands of secret agents bring,
as if they were the nations' conscience, honor, law,
whole bunches of rose microphones . . .

Enough!
          This dream's a nightmare.
It's poisonous,
                    this sinister marmalade.
I may not be altogether normal,
but neither am I quite abnormal.

Publicity,
          stop your neon hissing!
My simple understanding is:
a spy will always be a spy,
Christ always will be Christ.

Original Russian Sources

WORKS BY YEVGENY YEVTUSHENKO

Stikhi Raznikh Let (*Poems of Various Years*). Moscow: 1959.
Yabloko (*Apple*). Moscow: 1960.
Vzmakh Ruki (*A Wave of the Hand*). Moscow: 1962.
Nezhnost (*Tenderness*). Moscow: 1962.
My Russia. Autobiographical article in *The Observer*, London, May 27, 1962.
Autobiographie Précoce (*A Precocious Autobiography*), first published serially in *L'Express*, Paris, February 3–March 21, 1963; then as a book in Paris, London (William Collins & Sons) and New York (E. P. Dutton & Co.), 1963; and a Russian language edition in Toronto, 1963, and in London (Flegon Press, 1965).
Antologia Russkoy Sovietskoy Poesii, Vol. II, Moscow, 1957. This anthology contains four Yevtushenko poems (pp. 597–604).

RUSSIAN TEXTS

The Russian texts in this volume have been reprinted from the following books: *Yabloko*, *Vzmakh Ruki*, and *Nezhnost*. *Vzmakh Ruki* reprints a number of earlier poems which had appeared in the poet's previous works—*Prospectors of the Future* (1952), *Third Snow* (1955), *The Highway of Enthusiasts* (1956), *Promise* (1957), and *The Bow and the Lyre* (Tbilisi, ?1958). Those poems which are not included in any of the above volumes have been reprinted from certain Soviet periodicals and magazines:

"Babii Yar," from *Literaturnaya Gazeta*, September 19, 1961; "The Heirs of Stalin," from *Pravda*, October 21, 1962; "Again at Zima Station," "No I Won't Take The Half," "People Were Laughing," all from *Yunost*, No. 9, September, 1963; "Ah, How Faltering My Speech," "Love's Maturity," "Nefertiti," "Other Times," all from *Moskva*, No. 2, February, 1964; "The Third Memory," from *Novy Mir*, No. 7, July, 1964; "Prologue" and "The Dead Hand of the Past," from transcriptions.

The original of the excerpt from "The Execution of Stenka Razin" given in the Introduction was printed in *Literaturnaya Gazeta*, March 3, 1964.

Notes

In his 1962 edition, Yevtushenko has revised some of his earlier poems by making cuts and insertions. This applies especially to poems such as "The Angry Young Men" and "Honey." Where possible, the 1962 versions have been followed.

Prologue

According to Yevtushenko, this poem was first published in an earlier volume of his *Obeshchanie* (*A Promise*), 1957. It has not been reprinted since, but Yevtushenko has read it on various occasions and also at Harvard in 1961. The present text is based on a transcription.

Yesenin, Sergey (1895–1925): a Russian poet of great lyrical power and of nostalgic and tragic tone, who committed suicide.

Moussorgsky, M. P. (1835–1881): the father of Russian music, who composed the original version of the opera *Boris Godunov*.

There's Something I Often Notice

Lines 25–28 of this poem are also to be found in a longer poem, "Whence Are You?" (1958) included in *Stikhi Raznikh Let*.

Envy

This poem appears in (1) Antologia, (2) *Stikhi Raznikh Let*, and (3) *Vzmakh Ruki*. Line 19 (*zlu nie proshchaya za ego dobro*) is the same in (1) and (3). In (2) it was changed to "*otstaivaiya pravdu i dobro*" (defending the truth and the good). The text here is that of (3).

Deep Snow

Nogin Square: in Moscow.

Weddings

The poem throws some light on Yevtushenko as a boy at Zima Station during the war years. It was printed in the same three volumes as *Envy*. Lines 47–48 vary as follows: in (1), *visyat na sten-*

khakh | lozungi, | chto Gitleru kaput; in (2), *letyat po stenam lozungi, | i s Russkim piyet Yakut*; and in (3), *letyat po stenam lozungi, | chto Gitleru kaput.* The present text (3) is the same as (1) except for the word *visyat* (hang), which has replaced *letyat* (fly).

I Don't Understand
GUM: The State Universal Store. The main department store in Moscow.

The visions of Malapaga: this far-from-obvious allusion refers to an early neo-realist film, *The Walls of Malapaga* (1949), directed by René Clément and starring Jean Gabin and Isa Miranda. When shown in the early 1950's in the Soviet Union, this film produced a deep impression on the younger intellectuals. A passage in Alla Ktorova's "anti-novel," *The Face of the Fire-Bird*, published in *Grani*, No. 56, 1964, confirms this impact: "First of all: whence, how, and since when, did this Apukhtin-like mood of 'swooning melancholy' begin? Since 1950, when they began to show Franco-Italian movies in Moscow. We would queue up for three hours to get into the Coliseum and the Central to see *Rome at Eleven O'Clock*, *The Walls of Malapaga*, or *Address Unknown* . . . These movies completely transformed us . . ."

The Concert
The first line of this poem is new; the remaining lines are from *Zima Station*, the long challenging poem printed in *Oktyabr*, No. 10, 1956. *The Concert* is printed as an autonomous poem in *Nezhnost*. In it Yevtushenko attacks the stagnation of certain aspects of Soviet life, including the arts.

Zima Station: Yevtushenko's birthplace, a small town station situated some 200 miles S.W. of Irkutsk on the Transiberian railway.

bogatyr: the champion, knight, or mighty man of Russian folklore.

When I Think of Alexander Blok
Alexander Blok (1882–1921): the famous Russian poet and Symbolist, author of *The Twelve* (1918). In many of his poems he evokes

the nostalgic and foreboding atmosphere of pre-Revolutionary St. Petersburg. Since the 1950's there has been a considerable revival of interest in his work.

A Career

"Tolstoy—Leo" is intended to be ironic. Russian literature has had three Tolstoys—A. K., A. N., and Leo. But only Leo was in any sense a Galileo.

The Angry Young Men

The *Vzmakh Ruki* version omits six lines: "I'm happy / to believe / in Lenin's truth, / to believe in the truth / of the hammer / and the sickle" (*Stikhi Raznikh Let*).

Moscow Freight Station

Scriabin, Alexander (1872–1915): famous Russian composer. After neglect, there has been revived interest in his work.

Astrakhan: a port town on the Volga delta.

Meitovtza and *Miitovtza*: in the Russian text, students respectively of the Moscow Institute of Energetics and the Moscow Institute of Engineering and Transport.

Remarque, Erich Maria (1897–): author of *All Quiet On The Western Front*. His later novels have exercised a considerable influence on the younger Soviet intellectuals.

Ryazan: ancient town on the River Oka, S.E. of Moscow.

Vologda: old provincial capital N.E. of Moscow.

Humor

Hodja-Nasr-ed-Din: in Turkish legend, a famous jester and hero of many pranks which have been recorded in a jest-book.

Winter Palace: residence of the Tsars in St. Petersburg until the Revolution of March, 1917. The seat also of Kerensky's government until the October Revolution. Since then a museum.

This poem has been used by Dmitri Shostakovich in his *Thirteenth Symphony*.

The American Nightingale

First in *Literaturnaya Gazeta*, August 24, 1961. Written at Harvard in April of the same year. Dated wrongly in *Vzmakh Ruki*.

Honey

First published in *Moskva*, No. 6, 1961. The *Nezhnost* version has a number of changes including the insertion of five new lines, beginning with "Will fix the price there," and ending with "to agree on a price."

Chistopol: a town on the River Kama in the region of Kazan.

The Railing

First in *Yunost*, No. 12, 1960; then in *Vzmakh Ruki*.

Hail in Kharkhov

First in *Moskva*, No. 6, 1961; then in *Nezhnost*. In line 19, the word *zhlob*, in Kharkhov dialect, means something like a nasty fellow or a small gangster or hoodlum.

Babii Yar

Babii: women's. *Yar*: word meaning cliff or steep bank. A place outside Kiev where thousands of Jews were slaughtered by the occupying Nazis. The poem first appeared in *Literaturnaya Gazeta*, September 19, 1961, and caused so much controversy it has not been republished since. But it has been one of Yevtushenko's favorite reading pieces. Shostakovich has used the poem in the opening movement of his *Thirteenth Symphony*.

Alfred Dreyfus (1859–1935): a French artillery officer of Jewish descent who was sent to Devil's Island in 1894 for allegedly betraying military secrets. By 1914 he was finally cleared of the charges.

Meshchanin: Philistine. A favorite Russian expression of contempt for one of a "petty bourgeois mentality."

Byelostok: a town now in Soviet Byelo-Russia near the Polish frontier, which used to have a large Jewish population.

"The Union of the Russian People": an ultra-nationalist organization under Tsarism. It was responsible for the "Black Hundreds" — gangs which carried out Jewish pogroms.

Poetry

Kutuzov: the Russian Commander-in-Chief during the Napoleonic invasion. His strategy of retreat and delay helped to destroy the Grande Armée.

A Knock On The Door

First in *Literaturnaya Gazeta*, August 24, 1961, and, in English, in *Encounter*, No. 115, April, 1963. The present version from *Nezhnost* is four lines shorter. The cut was made after line 6.

Conversation With An American Writer

First appeared under the title of *A Talk* in the Kiev Ukrainian-language *Literaturna Gazeta*, December, 1961, and then in the Warsaw *Polytika* which had also published *Babii Yar*. Under its present title was published in *Nezhnost*.

The Heirs of Stalin

Appeared in *Pravda*, October 21, 1962. To date has not been reprinted in any of Yevtushenko's books.

Ryazan and Kursk: provincial capitals to the S.E. of Moscow.

Turksib and Magnitka: the new Turkestan-Siberian railway and the giant metallurgical combine, which were constructed as part of the Five Year Plan.

Enver Hoxha: the pro-Stalinist leader of the Albanian Communist Party.

I'm An Angel

Shchipachev, Stepan: a rather innocuous Soviet lyrical poet of bucolic mood and conservative sentiments, who has also written many love lyrics—until recently not the thing to do.

Again At Zima Station

The entire poem is about 300 lines. The two passages in this text describe the poet's return to *Zima* and some of his reflections on his fall from grace. The obvious comparison is with the first *Zima* poem published in 1956.

Klintzi: typifies any stagnant provincial town.

preference: a game of cards.

Yesenin, Sergey: in some of this poet's lyrics there are tender references to his mother.

Nefertiti
Nefertiti (1390–1354 B.C.): wife of 18th Dynasty Pharaoh Amenhotep IV. Immortalized in the bust now at Berlin Dahlem Museum.

Avicenna (980–c1036): Arab philosopher who had absorbed Aristotle and who, in turn, influenced mediaeval European thought.

The Woman And The Sea
From *Nezhnost*. The English version first printed in *The New Russian Poets* (henceforth referred to as NRS), N.Y., 1966.

Fears
From *Kater Svyazi* (*The Mail Boat*). *Molodaya Gvardia*. M. 1966. The English text first printed in Harper's Magazine, March, 1967.

The Song Of The Overseers
From the long loosely strung cycle entitled *Bratskaya GES* (*The Hydroelectrical Station at Bratsk*), printed in *Yunost*, No. 4, 1965. Also in NRS.

"Yes" and "No"
From *Yunost*, No. 6, 1965. Also in NRS.

Cinderella
From *Kater Svyazi*.

The Sigh
From *Den Poesii*. M. December, 1965. Also in *Kater Svyazi*.

Italian Tears
From *Novy Mir*, No. 6, 1966. Also in Atlas Magazine (N.Y.), January, 1967.

Impressions Of The Western Cinema

From *Ogonyok*, No. 30, September, 1966. The English version appeared in Atlas Magazine, January, 1967. Previously it was read in New York and elsewhere during Yevtushenko's tour in the United States in November-December, 1966.

Accatone: in Italian the word means "beggar." It is also the name of the "hero" after whom the film is ironically titled. Accatone is no ordinary beggar, but rather a loafer, sponger and pimp who lives in Rome on the edge of society and is at odds with the police. He is finally crushed by a car. The part was played by a non-professional, Franco Citti, who had himself been much involved with the police. The film was directed by Pier Paolo Pasolini and was released in Italy in 1961. To date, it has not been shown in the U.S.A.

Peons: a reference, perhaps, to Eisenstein's film *Que Viva Mexico!* (1934).

Malina: literally a raspberry or a raspberry bush; idiomatically, in the text, something like a "bowl of cherries."

Mao . . . Mao . . .: in the Russian text, as it first appeared in *Ogonyok*, this passage reads "Miaou . . . Miaou . . ."—a censor's ingenious and, indeed, amusingly diplomatic way of circumventing the political implications of the poet's real intention.

"*Your uncle strict in his demeanor*": an ironic use of a direct quotation, i.e. of the opening line (*"Moy dyadia/samikh chestnikh pravil"*) of Chapter I of Alexander Pushkin's famous narrative poem *Yevgeny Onegin*.

G. R.